HOW MUCH LONGER LIVE WOMEN THAN MEN AROUND THE GLOBE?

Astonishing Differences between Countries

PAVLE SICHERL

Gaptimer Report No. 2

Copyright © 2014 Pavle Sicherl

Ljubljana, February 2014

Layout and Figures: Jaka Hajnšek

Printed by CreateSpace, An Amazon.com Company.

ISBN 978-1495398834

FOREWORD

Inequalities between and within countries are a major problem of the current world situation, gender disparity is one of these issues. This report concentrates on gender disparity in life expectancy at various levels (at the world level for 196 countries and some aggregates; for EU27 countries with 269 NUTS2 regions, and draws conclusion also from the study of more than 3000 USA counties). The statistical results show the gender disparity in life expectancy is so much in favour of women thus standing out against so many domains where the gender disparity is in many countries leaning in the other direction. However, analysing this gender gap of life expectancy the main focus is on the striking differences between countries around the globe.

The book offers new insights by examining gender disparity in life expectancy by using the novel generic time distance methodology. The art of handling different views of data is crucial for discovering the relevant patterns and for providing a broader framework for policy and business analysis. Sustainable development is by definition a long-run and multi-dimensional phenomenon. Semantics of discussing the issues, in setting the targets and in the implementation should not be based only on static measures; it needs to be complemented by dynamic measures. This methodology presents an innovation that goes beyond the present state-of-the art in measuring the degree of inequality thus increasing the understanding of the situation in the time perspective.

Time distance methodology can be very helpful both in the preparation of the post-2015 agenda as well as in the continuous monitoring of implementation of selected indicators later, both on the aggregate and national levels. It is a generic methodology, applicable to many domains beyond gender disparity and many indicators beyond life expectancy.

Potential users of this methodology could be international and national organizations, NGOs, experts, businesses, managers, educators, students, interest groups, media, and the general public at the world, national, and sub-national levels.

This analysis of gender inequality in life expectancy deals mostly with the first part of the statement of Aristotel, "Let us first understand the facts, and then we may seek the cause". Namely, the multiple factors behind the astonishing magnitude of country differences in the gender gap in life expectancy are very complex and interconnected; they include medical, social, and economic factors requiring large systematic research project(s).

Ljubljana, February 2014   Pavle Sicherl

3

TABLE OF CONTENTS

Chapter 1

INTRODUCTION

Gender disparity is one of the important issues as inequalities between and within countries are major problems of the current world situation. This report concentrates on gender disparity in life expectancy at various levels (at the world level for 196 countries and some aggregates; for EU countries and NUTS2 regions, and draws conclusion also from the study of more than 3000 USA counties). This focus is complemented with a brief background analysis of disparities in the world for female and male life expectancy between countries and regions against the respective benchmarks together with the broad trends of increase over time. Co-financing of the Slovenian Science Foundation is gratefully acknowledged.

The study looks at two major points: that female life expectancy at birth is higher than that for males for 99.5 percent of the world population, on the one hand and that there is an astonishing great dispersion of this gender difference among countries, on the other. Two major statistical sources used are The UN World Population Prospects (The 2010 Revision) for the period 1950–2010 and Eurostat databases. Yet the main focus is to convey from these data additional insights and understanding by using a novel generic time distance methodology. Namely, measurement is costly and it is important to exploit existing data efficiently for building knowledge and for policy debate. Describing and perceiving inequalities in terms of percentages and ranks is not the end of the story. Development processes take place in time, and time is important as an operational and comparative metric.

The statistical picture of disparities is presented by using three descriptive measures (absolute and relative static measures as well as S-time-distance measure as a special family of time distance measures defined for the level of the indicator). Expressed in time units, the time distance approach is easy to understand and provides a useful complement to existing mostly static methods providing new insights from existing data.

The statistical results are raising questions for further analysis of the reasons that the gender disparity in life expectancy is so much in favour of women around the globe in contrast to fields where the gender disparity is in many countries very much tilted in the other direction. This article also contributes some novel methodological tools that can be usefully applied for other indicators in analysing gender and other disparities, both at macro and micro levels.

Chapter 2 deals with the methodology issues, elaborating on time distance measure as an additional perspective in analysing time-series data and in measuring inequalities. Empirically, the degree of disparity may be very different in static terms and in time distance, which leads to new conclusions and semantics important for policy considerations. The approach is universal, expressed in time units easily understandable by everyone, and applicable to a wide variety of fields at both the macro and micro levels. Since time distance view provides an additional dimension of temporal disparity, results by other methods are left unchanged but new conclusions can be reached.

In Chapter 3 the analysis of disparities in life expectancy in the world between countries, separately for men and for women, are measured both by static measures and S-time-distance to build a multidimensional perception of the degree of disparities in this domain before turning to gender disparities. For females median value of S-time-distance lag behind Sweden amounted to 46 years, which means that about 98 countries lagged Sweden by more than that; 20 countries even more than 110 years.

Gender disparities in life expectancy at birth in Chapter 4 showed that the unweighted average for 196 countries the female-male differences in life expectancy amounted to 4.6 years, and S-time-distance for the world average (i.e. the horizontal gap between trends of female and male life expectancy) for 2008 amounted to 20 years, 28 years for the EU27 and 35 years for the USA. The astonishing differences between countries for gender inequality in life expectancy are shown by comparing the respective world ranks of a country for females and males. The extreme negative differences of more than 50 ranks are shown in three Baltic countries, e.g. the rank of Estonia against the international frontier for females was 51, while the corresponding rank for males was 110. On the other extreme, e.g. the rank for Qatar was 65 for females and only 12 for males.

For a smaller number of EU27 countries we can undertake more detailed analysis in Chapter 5. A part of the EU material was published earlier in the journal IB Revija (Sicherl, 2013b) and I am grateful for the agreement to use it here. Analysis of the gaps behind the international frontier of ten best countries in the world is presented for the EU27 countries showing the time matrix as an innovative complementary approach for looking at time-series data. The time matrix provides a good summary overview over many units and years and also a first-level visualisation tool. Beyond that, time matrix enables one way of estimating two statistical measures, S-time-distance and S-time-step. The absolute gender difference varied from 3.7 years for the Netherlands to 11.2 years for Lithuania; in percentage terms it varies from around 5% to 16% of male life expectancy. For EU27 average the time delay for life expectancy of males behind females was at about 27 years; for five countries the time delay of male behind the female life expectancy is more than 50 years, i.e. more than half a century. The relationship is very persistent, it changes very slowly and the time distance shows the reality with new eyes. The situation is analysed also for 37 UK and 21 Italian NUTS2 regions.

This Gaptimer Report No. 2 on gender disparities in life expectancy around the globe is the next volume in the series of Gaptimer reports following the Gaptimer Report No. 1 (Sicherl, 2013a) 'World Inequalities in Human development Report (1980-2012)'.

Chapter 2

TIME DISTANCE PERSPECTIVE
LOOKING AND SEEING WITH NEW EYES

Methodology: Time distance measure as additional perspective in measuring inequalities

Time distance is an innovative approach for looking at time-series data. Expressed in time units, the approach is easy to understand, and provides new insights as a useful complement to existing mostly static methods. The approach is universal, understandable, and applicable to a wide variety of indicators and of fields of concern at both the macro and micro levels. Since time distance view provides an additional dimension of temporal disparity, results by other methods are left unchanged but new conclusions can be reached.

In our opinion a minimal analytical framework would consist of elements from two types of information (Sicherl, 2004):

1) Information about the present and intertemporal position of the observed unit, without regard to the position of other units. The level and the growth rate of the relevant welfare attributes can present this aspect.
2) Information about the position of the observed unit in relation to other units. Quantitative measures of static relative position (like absolute and relative differences, and for the case of many units Lorenz curve, Gini coefficient, Theil index, etc.) *have to be supplemented by time distance to incorporate the temporal relative position of a given unit with respect to compared units as an essential element of analysis.*

The descriptive statistical measures expressing disparities are predominantly static. The present state-of-the-art does not realise that, in addition to static comparison, there exists in principle a theoretically equally universal measure of difference (distance) in time when a given level of the variable is attained by the two compared time series.

A brief definition of two novel statistical measures: S-time-distance and S-time-step

The statistical measure **S-time-distance** measures the distance (proximity) in time between the points in time when the two series compared reach a specified level of the indicator X. For instance, Figure 6 shows that the world life expectancy of 66 years was attained by females in 1987 and by males in 2006, S-time-distance amounts to about 19 years (2006 minus 1987). This means that at the level of 66 years the male life expectancy was lagging in time for 19 years or that the female life expectancy was leading by 19 years. S-time-distance for a given level of X_L is defined as:

$$S_{ij}(X_L) = \Delta t(X_L) = t_i(X_L) - t_j(X_L) \qquad (1)$$

The **S-time-step** measures the time elapsed between two levels of a time-series, providing an alternative description of its growth rate, measuring the growth of a series by using the inverse relation to the conventional $\Delta X/\Delta t$ growth rate metrics. For instance, as shown in Figure 8 that world female life expectancy needed in the past about 3.4 years, and male life expectancy 3 years to increase the life expectancy from 65 years to 66 years. This is a complementary description of the dynamics of life expectancy to the conventional growth rate matrix, which would described the dynamics as about 0.4 percentage per year. Both measures are valid description of the dynamics of change, while for general public S-time-step might be even easier to understand. S-time-step is expressed in units of time and is defined as:

$$S_i(\Delta X_L) = [t_i(X_L + \Delta X) - t_i(X_L)]/\Delta X \qquad (2)$$

Further information on the time distance methodology and applications are available in numerous earlier publications like Kyklos (Sicherl, 1973), IB Revija (Sicherl, 1999), Social Indicators Research (Sicherl, 2007), in the paper published by OECD Statistics Directorate (Sicherl, 2011), and most extensively in the book 'Time Distance in Economics and Statistics' (Sicherl, 2012).

Static measures of disparity require no further explanation. Time distance methodology is well positioned to complement them as one of the appropriate tools for the task of measuring disparity. It provides two novel generic descriptive statistical measures to measure the time dimension of these disparities. The time distance approach brings about two persuasive advantages for extensive practical use. Expressed in time units it is intuitively understood by policymakers, professionals, managers, media, and the general public thus facilitating their subjective perception about their position in the society and in the world in this additional dimension. Another technical and presentation advantage is that time and time distance is comparable across variables, fields of concern, and units of comparison. This makes it an excellent analytical, presentation, and communication tool.

Gender inequality in life expectancy – static distance and time distance

Time series can be compared in two dimensions. In Figure 1 we take the example of the gender disparities in life expectancy at birth for EU27 aggregates. One way is to compare time series at the given point in time, i.e. in our case the static gap in life expectancy between women and men in 2010. The absolute difference amounts to 5.9 years; the index is 107.7. Another dimension of the degree of disparity is taking into consideration the distance in years when men and women reached the same reference level of the variable, in our case the life expectancy for men in 2010 was reached by women already in 1983 (i.e. 27 years earlier): S-time-distance amounted to 27 years.

Figure 1 illustrates these two dimensions of gender disparities in life expectancy. It shows that perceptions of the size of this gap can be very different depending on the statistical measure used. Here the static difference between two lines in 2010 is less than 8 percent (which may appear to be small) while the S-time-distance is around 27 years (which gives a very different perception of the magnitude of the gap). For realistic evaluation of the situation we need both measures.

The perception of wellbeing and of the degree of disparity is subjective. As shown empirically the degree of disparity may be very different in static terms and in time distance, which leads to new conclusions and semantics important for policy considerations. Different people will give different subjective weights to the static and time distance dimension of disparity and they might be also very different for different indicators. Further discussion on inter-temporal aspect of wellbeing will be available in Sicherl (in press). Different people will give different subjective weights to the static and time distance dimension of disparity and they might be also very different for different indicators.

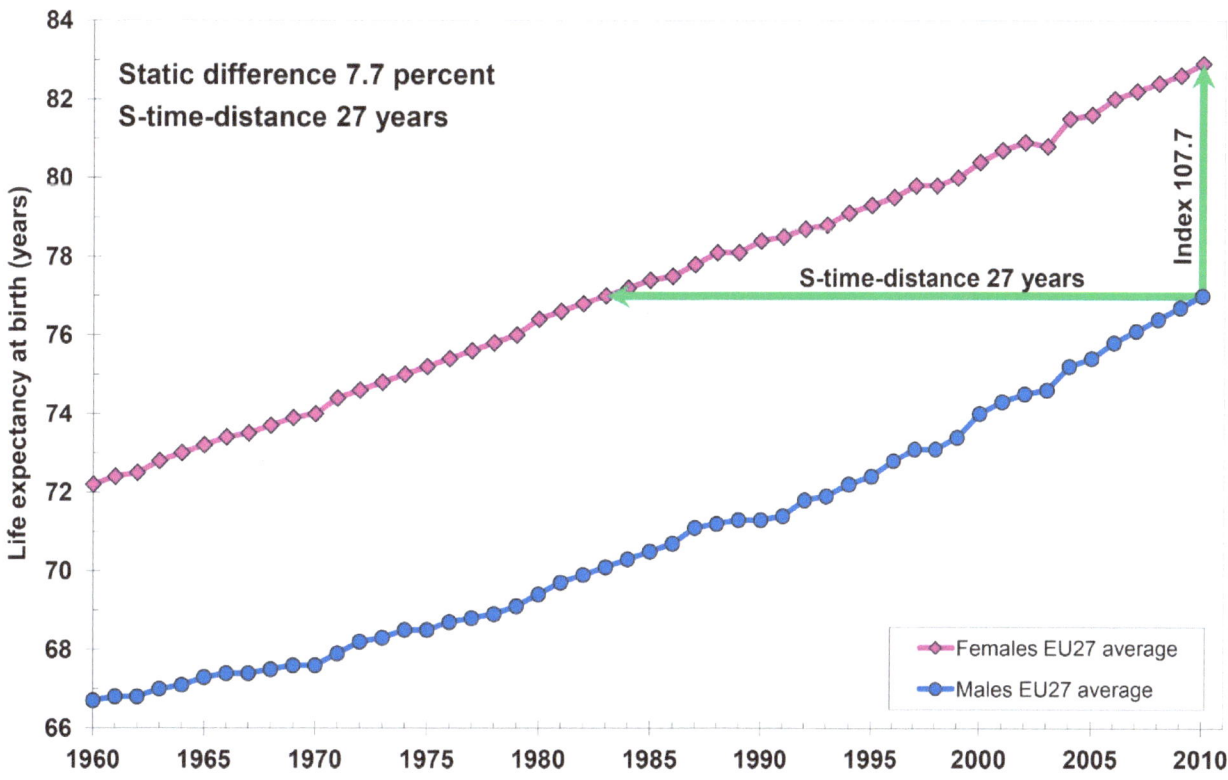

FIGURE 1 Gender disparities in life expectancy at birth, EU27 average in 2010: static index and time distance

SOURCE: Own calculations based on Eurostat (2006, 2013a).

Time distance is an innovative approach for looking at time-series data providing a broader dynamic analytical framework, complementing rather than replacing the existing mostly static measures. It is a generic approach, expressed in time units, easy to understand. There are several methods of calculating time distances and comparing them also with static measures, for three types of comparisons: the level of the indicators, their dynamics, and comparisons of levels relative to a benchmark (see Sicherl, 2011 and 2012). Another application not discussed here is time distance monitoring of implementation of targets. The Guardian published on their Global development web site my article on time distance method of measuring implementation of MDGs (Sicherl, 2013c).

Sicherl (2011: 9) explains in Table 1 the correspondence between the conventional table-format for time-series data, and the complementary presentation based on the time distance approach. It refers to three types of comparisons: the level of the indicators, their dynamics, and comparisons of levels relative to a benchmark.

This schematic presentation shows the correspondence between conventional table format as the starting point in the database and possible additional complementary presentation by time distance approach. The intention is to complement rather than replace the existing mostly static measures to provide a broader dynamic analytical framework.

One of these methodological possibilities is time matrix visualisation over many units and over time. Thus the first complementary presentation refers to the initial data for indicators. For presentation of levels the conventional table-format for time-series data is transformed into time matrix, which has a table-graph format. The identifiers in level-time matrix are units and selected levels of indicator while the corresponding times are in the main body of the table. Calculating these times by interpolations may pose a small problem of the degree of accuracy compared to original data but it gains additional understanding about time dimension of disparities and a good summary overview.

In the time matrix data are arranged by selected levels of indicators showing in which year these levels of the indicators were achieved by given country. This format of level-time matrix is easily understood by everybody, at the same time it provides also a simple visualisation tool for many units over time.

This allows for a quick level comparison:
- of the situation across the selected countries
- of how many steps over levels of indicators a given country has progressed, which is an additional indication of the dynamics in the country.

The use of time-matrix presentation to complement the usual time-series data tables covering many years and units shows that time matrix condenses such information in much smaller number of entries, which is of great advantage for presentation over many units and over time.

PRESENTATION OVER MANY UNITS AND OVER TIME
(LONG-TERM)

A. Conventional table format as the base	**B. Possible additional complementary presentation**

1. DATA FOR INDICATORS (example: life expectancy)

Table

A1	Time			
	1960	...	...	...	**2011**
Countries (units)	Indicator values at specific point in time			

Level-time matrix or table-graph

B1	Indicator value			
	66	...	...	...	**85**
Countries (units)	Time when the selected indicator value was achieved			

2. DYNAMICS AND COMPARISON OF DYNAMICS

Table of growth rates or indices of dynamics

A2	Time			
	1961	...	...	...	**2011**
Countries (units)	Annual growth rate or index of dynamics			

S-time-step (in years)

B2	Indicator value			
	67	...	...	...	**85**
Countries (units)	Time needed to achieve next level of the selected indicator value			

3. COMPARISON OF LEVELS

Index: benchmark = 100 by years

A3	Time			
	1960	...	...	...	**2011**
Countries (units)	Index values by years			

S-time-distance (in years) from benchmark

B3	Indicator value			
	66	...	...	...	**85**
Countries (units)	S-time-distance (in years): - time lead, + time lag from benchmark			

TABLE 1 Schematic presentation of correspondence between conventional table format and additional complementary presentation in time distance approach
Source: Sicherl (2011 and 2012).

By itself (i.e. even without calculating the two statistical measures S-time-distance and S-time-step) such matrices can be used in publications, web pages, etc. as a first-level visualisation tool to 'turn statistics into knowledge' (Sicherl, 2011: 30).

The first comparison can start with time matrix visualisation of the selected indicator over many units and over time. There are several examples of time matrices in the report. Figure 6 shows time matrix for female and male life expectancy for the world level and selected world regions (including S-time-distances between them for a given level of the life expectancy). Figure 13 shows time matrix for female life expectancy for EU27 countries, while Figure 16 for EU27 shows a combined large time matrix for all countries for both genders.

The second complementary presentation refers to dynamics and comparison of dynamics. Table of growth rates or indices of dynamics are complemented with table of S-time-step in Figures 8 and 15, which represent time needed to achieve the next level of the selected indicator value.

The third complementary presentation refers to comparison of levels. The index values by years (benchmark=100) is complemented in by the S-time-distance measure in years from the benchmark (– time lead, + time lag from benchmark). S-time-distances for selected levels of X_L are arrived at by subtracting the respective times for a given unit and the times for the benchmark unit. Time distance perspectives of inequalities are the focus of analysis in the book.

There are several forms of presentation of S-time-distances, e.g. Figures 2, 3, and 4 of values for about 196 countries behind the long-term trend of Sweden as benchmark; Figure 7 for selected world regions from benchmark China; Figures 14 and 18 against the benchmark of international frontiers as well as Figures 20 and 21 about disparities of regional values in the UK and Italy. International frontiers were defined as the average of the top 10 performers in the world according to data in UN (2011) for the respective gender for a given point in time.

There are several methods for calculating S-time-distances and S-time-step. One interesting approximate method is calculation of these two statistical measures from the respective time matrices. We can derive two statistical measures, expressed in standardized units of time (S-time-distance and S-time-step) by subtracting the respective times in the series between the compared units for a given level of the indicator or for each unit in the time matrix for consecutive levels of the variable, respectively. For instance, from time matrix in Figure 6 at the level of 67 years of life expectancy, this level was achieved by females around 1992 and males around 2009, subtracting these two times we get a rounded value of S-time-distance of about 18 years. From the same times in Figure 6 S-time-steps as a measure of dynamics are presented in Figure 8. For females the time needed in the past to increase one level of life expectancy 3.6 years were needed to increase life expectancy from 71 years to 72 years, and 3.4 years for males to increase life expectancy from 66 to 67 years.

Chapter 3

DISPARITIES IN LIFE EXPECTANCY IN THE WORLD

Time distance deviation for female and male life expectancy for 196 countries against the long-term trend of Sweden as the benchmark

In this chapter we analyse disparities in life expectancy in the world between countries separately for men and for women in the static and in time distance dimensions. This picture of world inequalities presents the background to better understanding of the analysis of gender disparity. Analysing the world disparities in life expectancy also in the time distance perspective can add new dynamic elements to understanding the magnitude of the degree of disparity in the world.

In Figure 2 S-time-distance in years is calculated for the 2005–2010 level of female life expectancy at birth in each of the 196 country. This is the difference in time between the current calendar year in these countries and the calendar year when the same level was achieved in Sweden in the past. Sweden was selected as the benchmark country because for Sweden long time series are available to cover a large range of historical development of one of the leading countries. In Figure 9 S-time-distances for overall life expectancy from benchmark Sweden are calculated for 13 selected countries over the period 1980-2012 (as distinct from 196 countries at a given point in time separately by gender in Figures 2 and 3). Also the world inequalities in life expectancy are very large indeed.

For females median value of S-time-distance lag behind Sweden amounted to 46 years, which means that about 98 countries lagged Sweden by more than that; 20 countries even more than 110 years. The static absolute difference between the current female life expectancy in Sweden and that of the median country is 7.7 years, percentage difference about 10 percent, S-time-distance is around 46 years. Again, relative static index of about 10% between Sweden and the median (98th) country does not give the perception of a large degree of world disparity in female life expectancy.

Median value of S-time-distance lag for males behind Sweden amounted to 58 years; 18 countries even more than 110 years. The static difference was 9.2 years, percentage difference about 12 percent, and time distance for the median more than half a century. Time distance lens brings additional perception of the magnitude and persistence of the world disparities in this indicator for females.

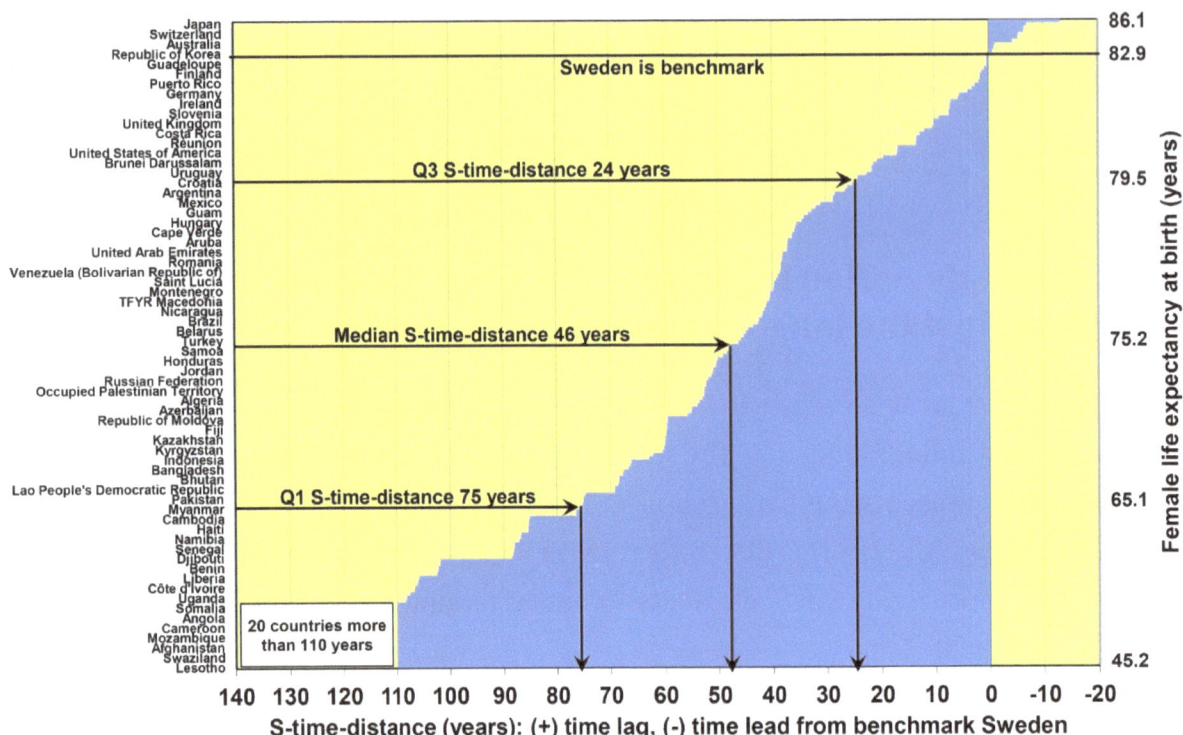

FIGURE 2 S-time-distance for female life expectancy at birth for 196 countries in 2005–2010 showing how many years earlier such level was attained in the long-term trend of Sweden as the benchmark

NOTE: Because of the high number of countries included, on the vertical axis only every third country name is shown.
SOURCE: Own calculations based on data from UN (2011); Human Mortality Database (2006) for Sweden.

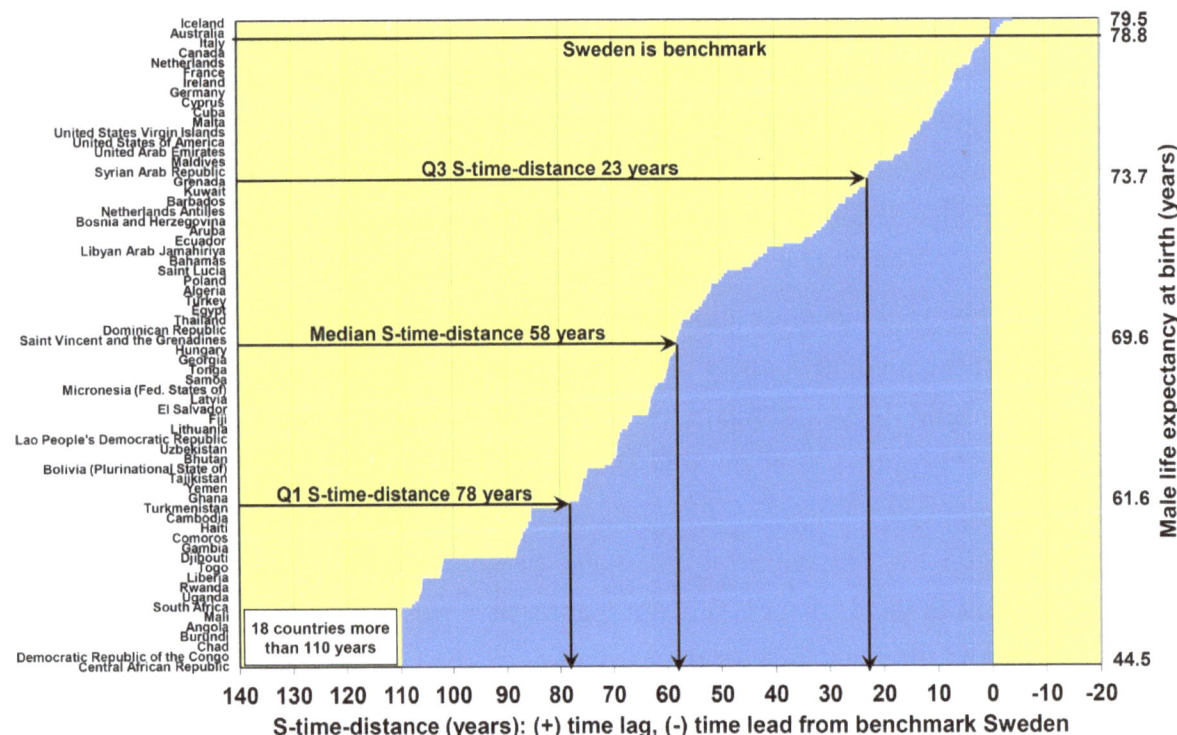

FIGURE 3 S-time-distance for male life expectancy at birth for 196 countries in 2005–2010 showing how many years earlier such level was attained in the long-term trend of Sweden as the benchmark

NOTE: Because of the high number of countries included, on the vertical axis only every third country name is shown.
SOURCE: Own calculations based on data from UN (2011); Human Mortality Database (2006) for Sweden.

The overall conclusion about the trends for the world can be also calculated as absolute difference and time distance in life expectancy by gender between the value for the world aggregate and the respective international frontier of the best 10 countries. Combining static (absolute) and time distance measures of the disparities in the life expectancy in the world we can reach a more complete picture of the situation.

To assess the summary degree of disparity in life expectancy in the world we can use three distances between the respective international frontier and the world average for the period 2005–2010:

- for females the absolute difference shows that the international frontier is around 14 years higher than the world average, in percentage terms about 16 percent higher, and in time distance measure the world average is more than 55 years behind the international frontier;
- for males the absolute difference is around 13 years, in percentage terms about 17 percent, and in time distance the world average is more than 55 years behind the international frontier.

Comparing time distances in life expectancy with other indicators

Sicherl (2012: 156–160) showed that time distance gap can be very illustrative also for comparisons of the dynamic degree of disparities across indicators from different domains. The median value of S-time-distance behind benchmark Sweden for GDP per capita was 74 years in 2008 using long-term data from Maddison (2010). One half of the countries (80 countries) were lagging Sweden at least that much (26 countries even for more than 150 years). A conventional statistic measure of world disparity Gini coefficient would be around 0.53, which is very difficult to understand and to explain to politicians and to the general public. Both measures are valid, yet the present state-of-the-art neglects the additional easily understandable perspective of time distance information available in time series databases and thus leads to an information loss that has no justification.

A very different perception of the overall degree of disparity than those for GDP per capita or life expectancy is that of some ICT indicators. International Telecommunication Union (ITU) in Geneva used the time distance measure for measuring the digital divide to show the difference in years between the 2008 level of mobile telephone penetration in each country and the year when the same level was achieved in Sweden (ITU, 2010: 43–52). Sweden was the natural choice for benchmark as Sweden was ranking first for the ICT Development Index (IDI) for 2008 and 2007. For mobile penetration rate the median value of S-time-distance lag for 200 countries behind Sweden was 7.5 years though the static differences were much larger than for life expectancy. The observed empirical large discrepancy between measures of disparity in the static and in the time dimensions confirms the theoretical conclusions that perceptions of disparities might be very different depending on the measure used. The greater the difference in the growth rates of the indicators, the greater is the possibility of such divergence.

Hosseinpoor et al. (2012) analysed differences between countries/regions and the top 5th percentile of life expectancy worldwide calling this international shortfall inequality. They concluded that these shortfall inequalities among men and among women decreased between 1950 and 1975 but stagnated thereafter. For women this shortfall started at 21 years and fell to 14.4 years by 1975 and stayed around that level until 2010.

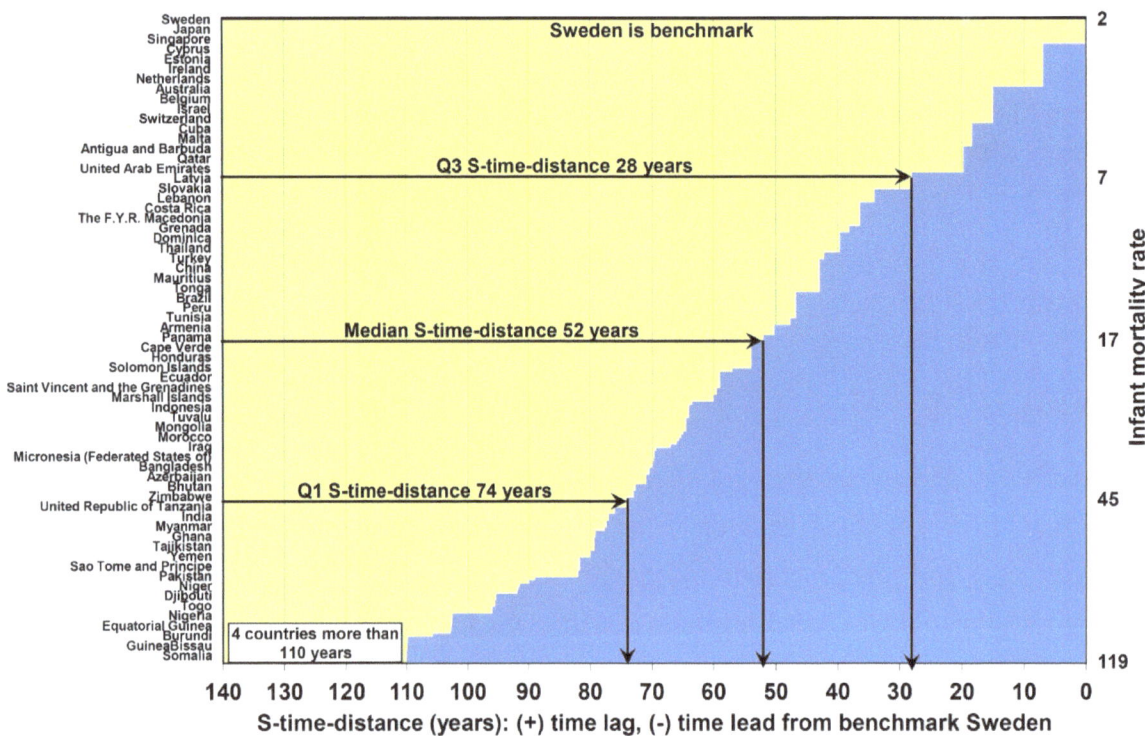

FIGURE 4 S-time-distance for infant mortality rates for 195 countries in 2011 showing how many years earlier such level was attained in the long-term trend of Sweden as the benchmark
NOTE: Because of the high number of countries included, on the vertical axis only every third country name is shown.
SOURCE: Own calculations based on data from UNICEF (2013); Mitchell (2003) and Eurostat (2013b) for Sweden.

Figure 4 provides another example of world inequalities in the time perspective. S-time-distance behind the long-term trend for Sweden shows very similar time dimension as in Figures 2 and 3 for gender life expectancy: median S-time-distance for 195 countries in 2011 amounts to 52 years. Also, S-time-distances for the lowest quarter of countries were behind the trend for Sweden from 74 to 78 years in the three Figures 2, 3, and 4.

Chapter 4

GENDER DISPARITIES IN LIFE EXPECTANCY
Static differences and time distances in life expectancy at birth between women and men

Gender inequalities for world aggregates and selected countries

At the world level we are using data from the UN (2011), World Population Prospects: The 2010 Revision, Estimates 1950–2010 with Medium-fertility variant 2010–2100. Figure 5 presents the difference in life expectancy between females and males over the whole period for four major aggregates: world, more developed regions, less developed regions, and least developed countries according to UN classification.

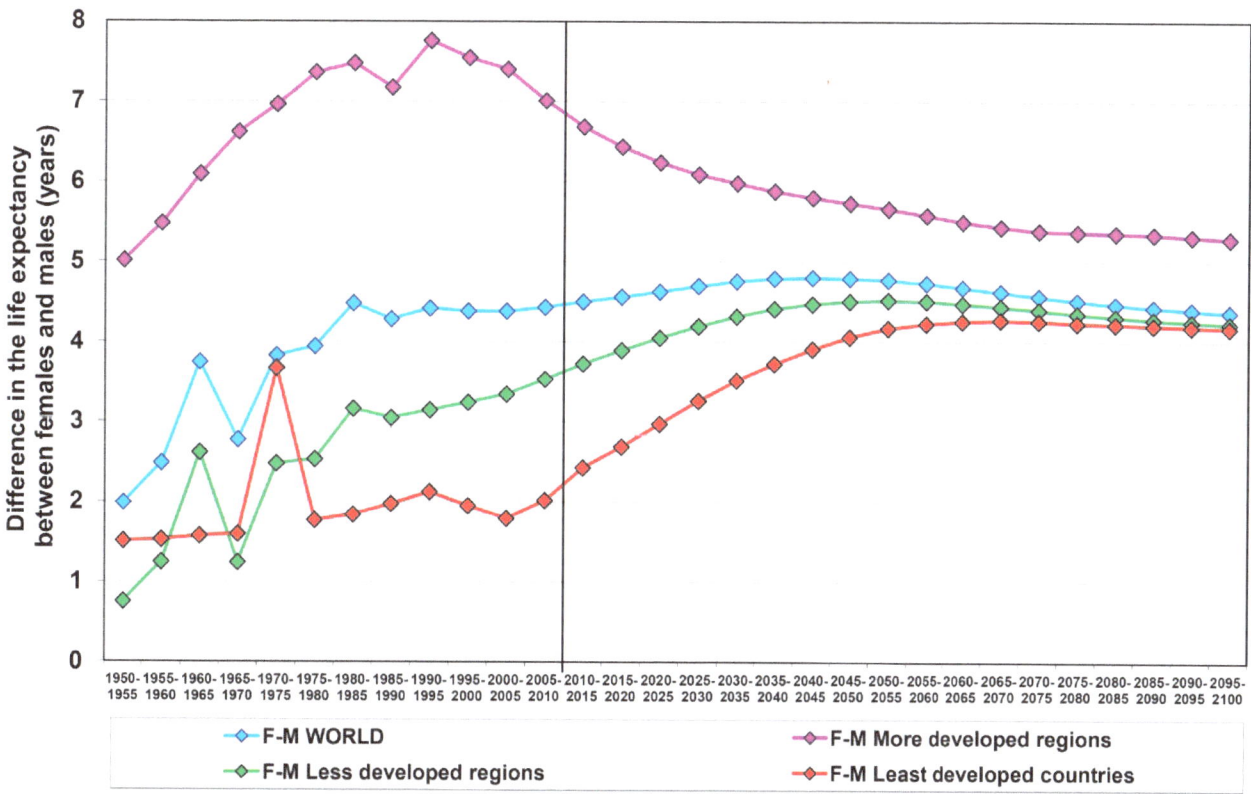

FIGURE 5 Difference in life expectancy at birth between females and males for four major world aggregates

SOURCE: Calculations based on UN (2011).

At a glance it can be observed that in the period from 1950–1955 to 2005–2010 the gender disparity in life expectancy in favour of women was much higher in the more developed regions (MDR) than in the less developed regions (LDR). While the expression 'More developed regions' and 'Less developed regions' might not be the correct expression of the development trends in the world we are following the UN classification to take advantage of their data. In this source MDR comprise Europe, Northern America, Australia/New Zealand, and Japan.

In the period 2005–2010 the range of absolute difference in life expectancy at birth between females and males ranges from 2 years for least developed countries to 7 years for more developed regions. Data for aggregates indicate a conclusion that the female-male disparity at life expectancy at birth is higher in more developed than in the less developed region. This conclusion might be rather different at country or regional level in some parts of the world discussed below. Medium-fertility variant for the future indicates that for the assumptions used it is expected that this range will narrow considerably; by 2070–2075 it is expected that the difference between the regions will come close to 1 year between the MDR and LDR as the difference between female and male life expectancy will amount to about 5 years for the MDR and about 4 years for the LDR. Without major changes in health conditions the UN estimates expect that the higher female than male life expectancy at birth is to be a condition to prevail over the period of 150 years.

The conclusion that the female life expectancy is higher than that for males is confirmed also at the country level for 97% of 196 countries in the above mentioned UN 2010 Revision. The countries with that exception vary. Only in the period 1950–1980 estimates show that Southern Asia (Afghanistan, Bangladesh, India, Iran, Maldives, and Nepal) experienced the situation that the life expectancy was higher for men than for women. In the period 2005–2010 this was true for only six countries, mostly in Africa (Zimbabwe, Lesotho, Botswana, Swaziland, Malawi, and Qatar; only a very small share of 0.5% of the world population). Life expectancy at birth is at present higher for females than for males in 99.5% of the world population.

Time	World	MDR	USA	EU27	LDR	China	India
1953	2.0	5.0			0.8	0.0	-1.7
1958	2.5	5.5			1.2	1.2	-1.8
1963	3.7	6.1	6.8	5.8	2.6	4.5	-1.7
1968	2.8	6.6	7.5	6.2	1.2	0.3	-1.4
1973	3.8	7.0	7.7	6.5	2.5	3.0	-1.1
1978	3.9	7.4	7.7	6.9	2.5	3.1	-0.2
1983	4.5	7.5	7.1	6.9	3.2	3.0	0.0
1988	4.3	7.2	6.9	6.9	3.0	3.1	0.2
1993	4.4	7.8	6.6	6.9	3.1	3.2	1.1
1998	4.4	7.5	5.7	6.7	3.2	3.3	1.7
2003	4.4	7.4	5.1	6.2	3.3	3.3	2.3
2008	4.4	7.0	5.0	6.0	3.5	3.4	2.9
2098	*4.4*	*5.3*			*4.2*	*3.9*	*3.8*

TABLE 2 Gender disparities in life expectancy in years (female minus male)

NOTE: Data in UN (2011) are presented by 5 years periods, for easier presentation and calculation we take middle year of period, e.g. 1988 refer to 1985–1990 period.
SOURCE: Based on data from UN (2011); for EU27 Eurostat (2012a); for USA OECD (2012).

Time	World	MDR	USA	EU27	LDR	China	India
1953							
1958					2.6		-3.0
1963	8.5				5.6		-2.7
1968	2.9				1.1	0.1	-2.2
1973	6.3				3.8	2.3	-1.8
1978	8.3				4.9	6.0	-0.4
1983	11.1	28.6			7.2	9.7	0.1
1988	12.6	31.2			8.5	11.2	0.5
1993	16.0	36.4			10.9	12.9	3.1
1994				34.0			
1995				34.0			
1996			36.0	33.0			
1997			33.3	32.5			
1998	18.7	39.8	33.0	33.5	13.3	14.8	4.1
2003	20.2	42.3	33.7	31.0	14.4	16.9	5.5
2008	20.2	41.5	34.7	28.0	13.3	17.2	7.1

TABLE 3 S-time-distance (in years): Time lag for males behind females life expectancy for a given level of males

SOURCE: Own calculations based on data from UN (2011); for EU27 Eurostat (2012a); for USA OECD (2012).

As we have seen in the example for the EU27 average in Figure 1 the time distance dimension of the gender disparity was very high. For the world average in the period 2005–2010 the S-time-distance was 20 years, which means that the level of male life expectancy in the period 2005–2010 was attained by females already in 1988. For the more developed regions S-time-distance amounted to about 41 years and for the less developed regions to about 13 years.

Time distances of gender inequalities in life expectancy at the global level

For a smaller number of EU27 countries we were able to perform more detailed analysis, with time matrix visualisation and derivation of the respective S-time-distances and S-time-steps in Chapter 5. For the much larger UN database of 196 countries it is simply impossible to go into such detail in the report. Figure 6 nevertheless presents an example how the time matrix visualisation can at a glance provide comparisons across gender within a group as well as comparisons of levels of either female or male life expectancy among different units shown in the figure

From the values in the time matrix it is possible to calculate S-time-distances for gender disparity (for male to female lag they are also presented in the third column for each group). The highest value of life expectancy achieved by both females and males in the world was 67 years. That level was achieved by females around 1992, by males around 2009, so that the S-time-distance amounted to about 18 years. The gender time gap for Western Europe was 27 years (at level 78), for Northern America 34 (at level of 76), for Latin America and the

Caribbean 22 years (at level 71), for China 11 years (at level 74), and for Africa 5 years (at level 57).

Level of life expectancy at birth (years)	WORLD			Australia/ New Zealand			Western Europe			Northern America			Latin America and the Caribbean			China			Africa		
	Females	Males	S-time-distance	Females	Males	S-time-distance	Females	Males	S-time-distance	Females	Males	S-time-distance	Females	Males	S-time-distance	Females	Males	S-time-distance	Females	Males	S-time-distance
84				2010																	
83				2004			2008														
82				2000			2003														
81				1996			1998			2009											
80				1991	2012	21	1993			2003											
79				1987	2007	20	1988			1991											
78				1981	2003	22	1984	2011	27	1982			2013								
77				1978	2001	23	1980	2006	26	1977			2009								
76				1975	1998	23	1976	2003	27	1974	2008	34	2005			2009					
75				1972	1995	23	1972	2000	28	1971	2004	32	2001			2004					
74				1960	1991	31	1966	1997	30	1966	1999	34	1997			2001	2012	11			
73				1955	1988	33	1961	1993	32	1958	1995	37	1994			1998	2006	7			
72	2011			1952	1984	33	1958	1988	31	1954	1990	37	1991			1995	2003	8			
71	2008				1981		1955	1984	29	1950	1984	33	1989	2011	22	1990	2001	11			
70	2004				1978		1952	1980	28		1979		1986	2007	21	1985	1999	13			
69	2001				1975			1976			1976		1984	2003	19	1981	1996	15			
68	1998				1970			1969			1973		1982	1999	18	1977	1990	13			
67	1992	2009	18		1953			1960			1968		1980	1996	17	1974	1986	12			
66	1987	2006	19					1955			1953		1978	1993	16	1972	1982	9			
65	1983	2003	19					1952					1976	1991	15	1971	1978	7			
64	1981	2000	19										1974	1988	14	1970	1975	4			
63	1978	1996	18										1971	1985	13	1970	1971	1			
62	1975	1989	13										1969	1982	13	1969	1970	1			
61	1973	1985	12										1967	1979	12	1969	1969	1			
60	1971	1982	11										1965	1976	11	1968	1969	1			
59	1969	1979	10										1963	1973	11	1968	1968	0	2011		
58	1968	1976	8										1961	1971	10	1967	1968	0	2010		
57	1967	1972	5										1959	1968	9	1967	1967	0	2008	2013	5
56	1966	1969	4										1957	1965	8	1966	1967	1	2007	2011	4
55	1965	1968	3										1955	1963	7	1966	1967	1	2005	2009	4
54	1963	1967	3										1954	1960	7	1966	1966	1	2002	2007	4
53	1962	1966	4										1952	1958	6	1965	1966	1	1985	2005	20
52	1961	1965	4										1951	1957	6	1965	1966	1	1982	2003	21
51	1959	1964	5											1955		1964	1965	1	1979	1999	19
50	1956	1963	7											1953		1964	1965	1	1977	1986	9
49	1954	1961	7											1951		1963	1965	1	1975	1982	8
48	1953	1958	5													1963	1964	1	1973	1980	7
47	1951	1954	3													1962	1964	2	1970	1977	7
46		1952														1961	1964	2	1968	1975	7
45		1951														1959	1963	4	1966	1972	7
44																1951	1963	12	1963	1970	7
43																	1962		1961	1968	6
42																	1961		1959	1965	6
41																			1957	1963	5
40																			1955	1960	5
39																			1953	1958	5
38																			1951	1956	5
37																				1954	
36																				1952	

Legend: Females   Males   S-time-distance (in years): Time lag of males behind females

FIGURE 6 Time matrix for selected units: female life expectancy, male life expectancy, S-time-distances between them for a given level of the life expectancy

SOURCE: Own calculations based on UN (2013).

However, in addition to that, one can also observe the time distances between units, not only between males and females for a given unit.

Figure 7 shows S-time-distance (years): time lead or time lag from benchmark China. China was selected as the benchmark as it has shown the highest increases in life expectancy at birth in the table. The level of 76 years for female life expectancy was attained in China in 2009, in Latin America and the Caribbean in 2005, in Northern America in 1974 and in Western Europe in 1976, and in Australia/New Zealand in 1975. Thus the time distance lag for China at that level of female life expectancy amounted to 4 years behind Latin America and the Caribbean, and between 32 and 34 years behind Western Europe, Northern America, and Australia/New Zealand.

For males the time distances of China behind the more advanced regions are smaller than of females. At the level of male life expectancy at 74 years, China arrived at that level in 2012, Northern America in 1999, Western Europe in 1997, and Australia/New Zealand in 1991. At that level male life expectancy was lagging behind Northern America for 13 years, behind Western Europe for 16 years, and behind Australia/New Zealand 21 years. For male life expectancy at birth China was, however, for selected levels 10 years ahead Latin America and Caribbean, 24 ahead of world average, and 46 years ahead of Africa.

It is interesting to observe the changing position of China during the analysed period. In the mid-1960s, at level of life expectancy for females of 57 years and of male value of 53 years, China crossed from the position of being below the world level to the being above that, increasing their lead against the world level to 16 years for women and for 24 years for men. The three advanced units in the table were always ahead of, and Africa behind, China.

Vertical comparisons show also at a glance the range of values achieved for a given unit over the period of available data. In absolute terms obviously the greatest increase was achieved in China, for both female and male life expectancy. It is remarkable that during 1960s the life expectancy was growing so fast that an increase of life expectancy of 1 year was achieved on the average in each six months period. Even Africa increased life expectancy for more years than the three most advanced units in the table, both in absolute and in relative terms, which confirms that at the higher levels life expectancy is more difficult to increase.

S-time-step as a measure of dynamics in Figure 8, showing the number of years needed to achieve the next level of the indicator, can be easily calculated by subtracting the years in each column for female or male life expectancy in Figure 6 (e.g., for females to increase life expectancy at the world level from 71 to 72 years 3.6 years were needed and for males to increase from 66 to 67 years 3.4 years were needed. At the highest level Australia/New Zealand needed about 5.5 years to increase the female life expectancy from 83 to 84 years, and for male life expectancy 5.6 years were needed for increase from 79 to 80 years).

Level of life expectancy at birth (years)	WORLD		Australia/ New Zealand		Western Europe		Northern America		Latin America and the Caribbean		China		Africa	
	Females	Males	Females	Males	Females	Males	Females	Males	Females	Males	Females	Males	Females	Males
80														
79														
78														
77														
76			-34		-32		-34		-4		0			
75			-32		-31		-32		-3		0			
74			-41	-21	-35	-16	-35	-13	-4		0	0		
73			-43	-18	-37	-13	-41	-11	-4		0	0		
72	16		-43	-18	-37	-15	-41	-12	-4		0	0		
71	18			-20	-35	-17	-39	-17	-1	10	0	0		
70	19			-21	-33	-19		-19	1	8	0	0		
69	20			-21		-20		-20	2	7	0	0		
68	20			-21		-21		-17	4	9	0	0		
67	18	24		-33		-26		-17	5	11	0	0		
66	14	24				-27		-28	5	12	0	0		
65	12	25				-26			4	13	0	0		
64	10	25							3	13	0	0		
63	8	25							2	14	0	0		
62	6	19							0	12	0	0		
61	5	16							-1	10	0	0		
60	3	13							-3	7	0	0		
59	2	11							-5	5	0	0	44	
58	1	8							-7	3	0	0	43	
57	0	5							-8	1	0	0	41	46
56	-1	3							-9	-2	0	0	40	44
55	-1	1							-11	-4	0	0	39	42
54	-2	1							-12	-6	0	0	37	41
53	-3	0							-13	-7	0	0	20	39
52	-4	-1							-14	-9	0	0	17	37
51	-6	-1								-11	0	0	15	33
50	-8	-2								-12	0	0	13	21
49	-9	-3								-13	0	0	11	18
48	-10	-6									0	0	10	15
47	-11	-10									0	0	8	13
46		-11									0	0	7	11
45		-12									0	0	6	9
44											0	0	12	7
43												0		5
42												0		4
41														
40														

Legend:
Females (time lead)　Males (time lead)　Females (time lag)　Males (time lag)

FIGURE 7 S-time-distance (years): (–) time lead or (+) time lag from benchmark China
SOURCE: Own calculations based on Figure 6.

Level of life expectancy at birth (years)	WORLD		Australia/ New Zealand		Western Europe		Northern America		Latin America and the Caribbean		China		Africa	
	Females	Males	Females	Males	Females	Males	Females	Males	Females	Males	Females	Males	Females	Males
84			5.5											
83			4.3		4.9									
82			4.5		4.9									
81			4.2		4.9		6.1							
80			4.3	5.6	4.7		11.6							
79			5.9	3.3	4.2		9.1							
78			3.3	2.7	4.0	4.3	4.7		4.3					
77			2.8	2.8	3.8	3.3	2.9		4.2					
76			3.5	3.3	4.1	3.2	3.1	4.9	3.8		5.0			
75			11.6	3.2	6.0	3.4	5.7	4.5	3.4		2.8			
74			5.0	3.1	5.3	3.8	7.9	4.2	3.1		2.5	6.5		
73			3.3	3.9	3.5	4.7	4.1	4.5	2.9		3.4	3.3		
72	3.6			3.8	2.8	4.1	3.3	6.8	2.7		5.4	2.0		
71	3.1			3.0	2.4	3.9		4.5	2.6	3.8	4.3	1.9		
70	3.1			3.1		4.4		2.9	2.4	3.7	3.8	2.5		
69	3.8			4.9		6.6		2.9	2.2	3.5	4.0	5.7		
68	5.8			16.9		9.2		4.9	2.0	3.1	3.4	4.7		
67	5.0	3.4				4.6		15.2	2.0	2.8	1.7	4.0		
66	3.4	3.0				3.6			2.0	2.9	1.2	3.7		
65	2.8	3.0							2.0	2.9	0.9	3.5		
64	2.6	4.0							2.1	2.8	0.7	3.4		
63	2.5	7.1							2.1	3.0	0.6	1.3		
62	2.4	3.9							2.2	3.2	0.5	0.8		
61	2.1	3.0							2.3	2.9	0.5	0.5		
60	1.7	3.1							2.2	2.6	0.4	0.5		
59	1.3	3.1							2.0	2.6	0.4	0.4	1.8	
58	1.1	3.4							1.8	2.7	0.4	0.4	1.6	
57	1.1	2.7							1.7	2.8	0.4	0.4	1.6	2.3
56	1.1	1.5							1.6	2.5	0.4	0.3	1.7	2.0
55	1.1	1.1							1.5	2.3	0.4	0.3	2.4	1.8
54	1.3	1.0							1.5	2.0	0.4	0.3	17.2	1.9
53	1.6	0.9							1.6	1.9	0.4	0.3	3.3	2.3
52	2.1	1.0								1.8	0.4	0.3	2.6	4.0
51	2.3	1.1								1.7	0.4	0.3	2.3	12.4
50	2.0	1.5								1.7	0.5	0.3	2.2	3.8
49	1.7	3.4									0.5	0.3	2.2	2.8
48	1.4	3.7									0.7	0.3	2.3	2.5
47		1.8									0.9	0.4	2.3	2.3
46		1.4									2.0	0.4	2.3	2.3
45											8.2	0.5	2.3	2.4
44												0.6	2.2	2.5
43												1.2	2.1	2.5
42													2.0	2.4
41													1.9	2.3
40													1.9	2.1
39													1.9	2.1
38														2.0
37														2.0
36														

Legend: Females   Males

FIGURE 8 S-time-step (years): time needed to achieve the next level of the life expectancy for males and females for selected units

SOURCE: Own calculations based on Figure 6.

Figure 9 (Sicherl, 2013a) is complementing conclusions about the magnitude of time distance gaps between females and males from the averages for Western Europe and Northern America to other units. It deals with overall life expectancy for 13 selected countries over the whole range of 187 countries from the Human Development Report (UNDP, 2013a) for the period 1980-2012 against the benchmark of life expectancy in history of Sweden.

HDI Rank	1	2	45	51	90	94	101	121	136	145	146	146	186	8
LEXP Level	Norway	Australia	Argentina	Uruguay	Turkey	Tunisia	China	Indonesia	India	Kenya	Pakistan	Bangladesh	Niger	Sweden
82														
81	3	-3												0
80	3	0												0
79	4	1												0
78	5	2												0
77	6	4		24										0
76	3	6	30	25										0
75		8	31	26										0
74			36	31	46	43								0
73			39	34	50	44	51							0
72			39	35	52	45	51							0
71			38	34	53	46	49							0
70			35		54	46	46							0
69					54	45	43	65				66		0
68					53	45	40	63				64		0
67					55	47	39	64				64		0
66					56	47		63				64		0
65					56	47		61	72		72	63		0
64					59	51		63	75		72	67		0
63					59	50		61	73		68	65		0
62					61			62	74		68	67		0
61					66			67	77		70	72		0
60					65			65	75		67	70		0
59					64			63	72	70	64	69		0
58					63			61	69	72	61	67		0
57					62				66	92		65		0
56									77	103		76		0
55										103			107	0
54										105			108	0
53										103			106	0
52													106	0
51													105	0
50													117	0
49													116	0
48													119	0
47													120	0
46													120	0
45													119	0
44													124	0
43													123	0
42													121	0
41													118	0
40													125	0

S-time-distance (in years): (-) time lead, (+) time lag from the benchmark Sweden

FIGURE 9 S-time-distances (in years) indicating lag or lead behind the benchmark of long-term trend for Sweden for total life expectancy
SOURCE: Own calculations based on data from UNDP (2013b), for Sweden before 1980 Mitchell (2003).

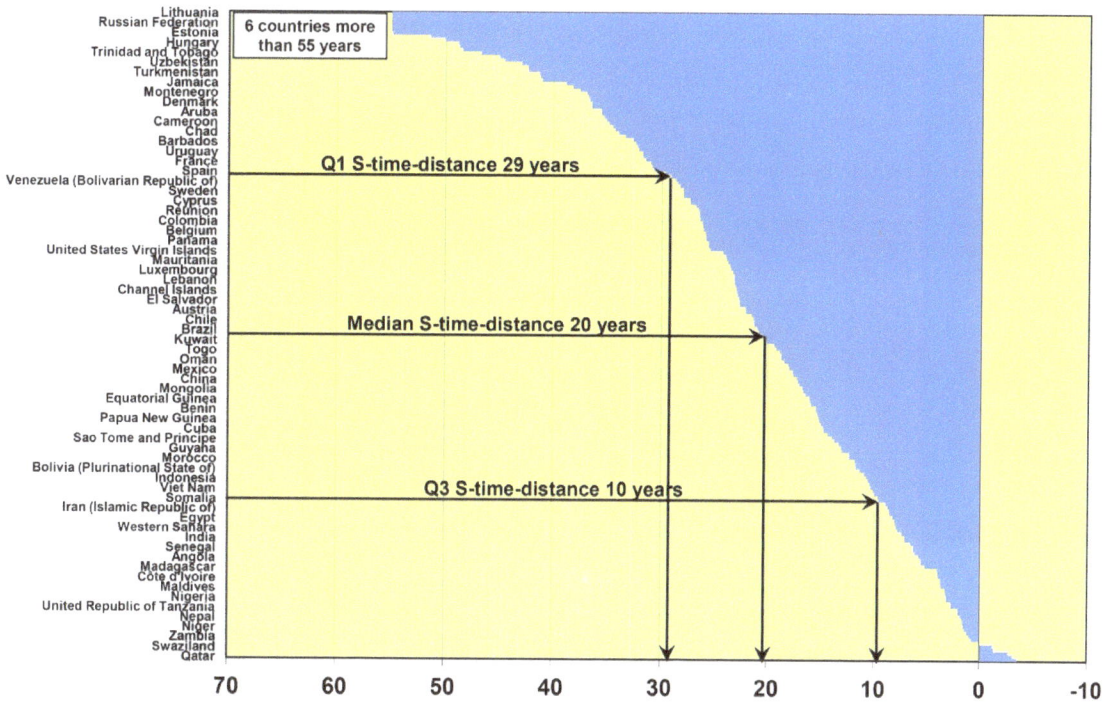

FIGURE 10 Time distance between male and female life expectancy at birth around 2005–2010 for 196 countries

NOTE: Because of the high number of countries included, on the vertical axis only every third country name is shown.
SOURCE: Own calculations based on data from UN (2011).

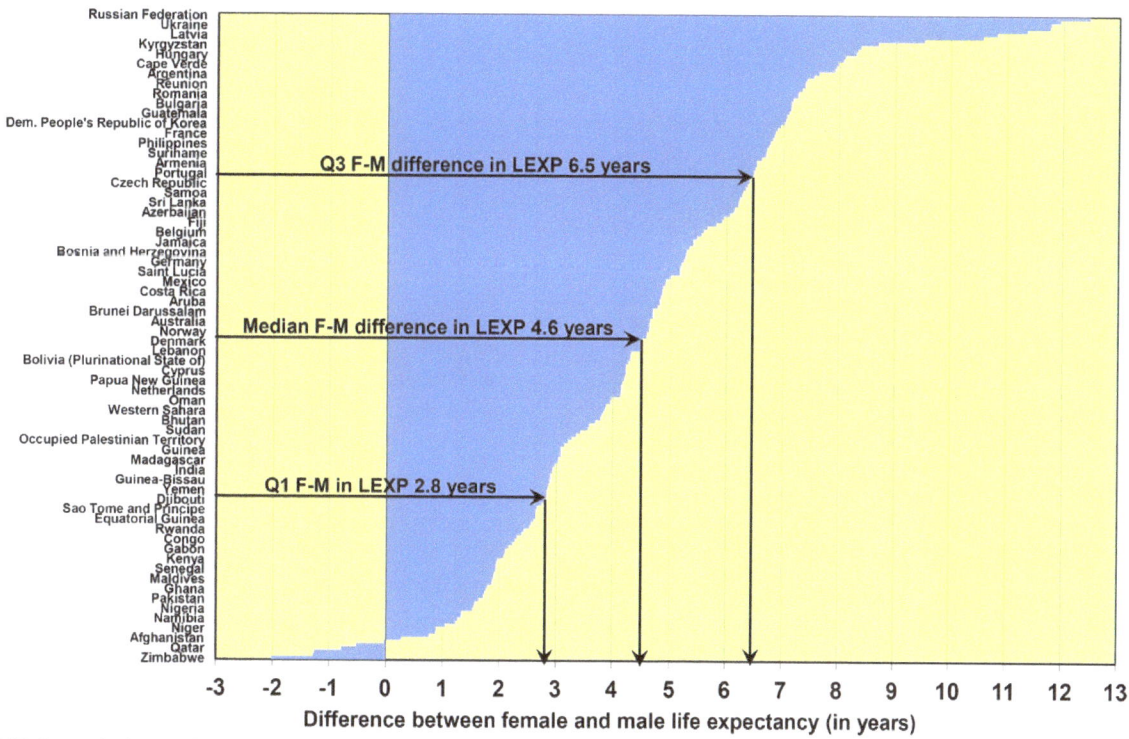

SOURCE: Own calculations based on data from UN (2011).

FIGURE 11 Absolute difference between female and male life expectancy at birth around 2005–2010 for 196 countries

NOTE: Because of the high number of countries included, on the vertical axis only every third country name is shown.
SOURCE: Own calculations based on data from UN (2011).

The time distance lag of male levels behind the same levels of female life expectancy can be further illustrated in Figure 9 over the whole range of 196 countries from the UN (2011) database. For each of these countries it was calculated how many years earlier were the 2005–2010 values of male life expectancy attained by female life expectancy in the same country The median S-time-distance amounted to 20 years, for about 98 countries the time lag was even higher than that. For 6 countries it was higher than 55 years, the 2005–2010 male value was lower than that for female in 1950–1955. Though the S-time-distances for the past should not be taken as prediction for the future these values indicate that the gender disparity in life expectancy is very persistent and will be in most countries very difficult to eliminate.

Different perception of inequality based on percentage and time distance measures

Different possible statistical measures can be used to describe the magnitude of inequalities. Below we are showing the comparison of the results for inequality in total life expectancy using three descriptive statistical measures: absolute difference, percentage difference, and S-time-distance.

Similar to the example in Figure 1 the cases in this table indicate that perceptions of the size of this gap can be very different depending on the statistical measure used. The static difference against Sweden was less than 10 percent for China and 11 percent for Lithuania (which may appear to be small) while the S-time-distance was 51 and 55 years, respectively (which gives a very different perception of the magnitude of the gap). The earlier comments showed how the time distance for the case for Niger behind Sweden was beyond 100 years, i.e. about twice of the above two countries.

Comparison	Absolute difference	Percentage difference	S-time-distance (years)
Sweden – China	7.9	9.7%	51
Sweden – Lithuania	9.1	11.2%	55
Sweden – Niger	26.5	32.5%	107

TABLE 4 The perception of the magnitude of the differences in total life expectancy may differ depending on the measure used
SOURCE: Own calculations based on data from UNDP (2013b), for Sweden before 1980 Mitchell (2003).

County levels USA

Institute for Health Metrics and Evaluation (IHME), University of Washington, Seattle, USA prepared a detailed analysis of life expectancy by gender for more than 3000 USA counties in the study "Falling behind: life expectancy in US counties from 2000 to 2007 in an international context" (Kulkarni et al., 2011).

This complex study presented the summary picture by showing the time distance (the number of calendar years that each of the more than 3000 USA counties was lagging behind or being ahead) against the 'international frontier' of ten best countries in the world. In the news release it was concluded that "Despite the fact that the US spends more per capita than any other nation on health, eight out of every 10 counties are not keeping pace in terms of health outcomes." (IHME, 2011) This application also demonstrates the telling power of time distance concept in presentation and visualisation.

Data presented in the web appendix of that study enabled us to look also at the female-male disparity in life expectancy similar to those in other sections of this report. In Table 5 it is shown that the median value for 3118 USA counties for female-male disparity in 2007 was 5.5 years, which is the same than the median value for NUTS2 regions for 2010, slightly less than for EU27 countries, and more than the median value for 196 world countries. Calculation for 2007 showed that in all of 3118 USA counties female life expectancy was higher than that of male life expectancy.

Comparing all five levels of analysis of gender disparities

Comparing all five levels of analysis of gender disparities it has been shown that that the values of absolute differences between female and male life expectancy are for quartiles similar for the EU and USA cases, while the coefficient of variation (defined as the ratio between standard deviation and the median) was larger in the EU than in the USA. However, the S-time-distances between the trends of levels of female and male life expectancy in 2008 were 28 years for the EU27 and 35 years for the USA; in both cases showing very substantial and persuading differences in favour of women in these two developed regions.

	World countries	EU27 countries	NUTS1	NUTS2	USA counties
	2005–2010	around 2010	around 2010	around 2010	2007
Number of units	196	27	97	269	3118
Range of absolute differences (years)	-2.0–12.5	3.9–10.9	3.8–10.9	2.3–10.9	2.7–11.1
Average females-males (years)	4.6 (4.4)	6.3 (5.9)	5.9	5.8	5.6
Q1	2.8	4.8	4.5	4.5	4.9
Q2	4.6	6.1	5.9	5.5	5.5
Q3	6.4	7.4	7	6.9	6.2
Coefficient of variation (KV %)	56%	32%	27%	28%	17%

TABLE 5 Gender disparities in life expectancy at the world, EU27, and regional EU and USA levels
NOTE: Values in brackets refer to the weighted values for the aggregate.
SOURCE: Calculation based on data from UN (2011); Eurostat (2012a, 2012b); Kulkarni et al. (2011).

Figure 5 showed that female-male difference in life expectancy was much higher in the aggregate for more developed regions than in the aggregate for less developed regions. However, this does not mean that higher income level should be considered as a single most important factor for the female-male difference. In Figure 12 the more detailed disaggregation of world regions of female-male differences in the 2005–2010 period is showing that the factors contributing to gender differences in life expectancy are much more complicated.

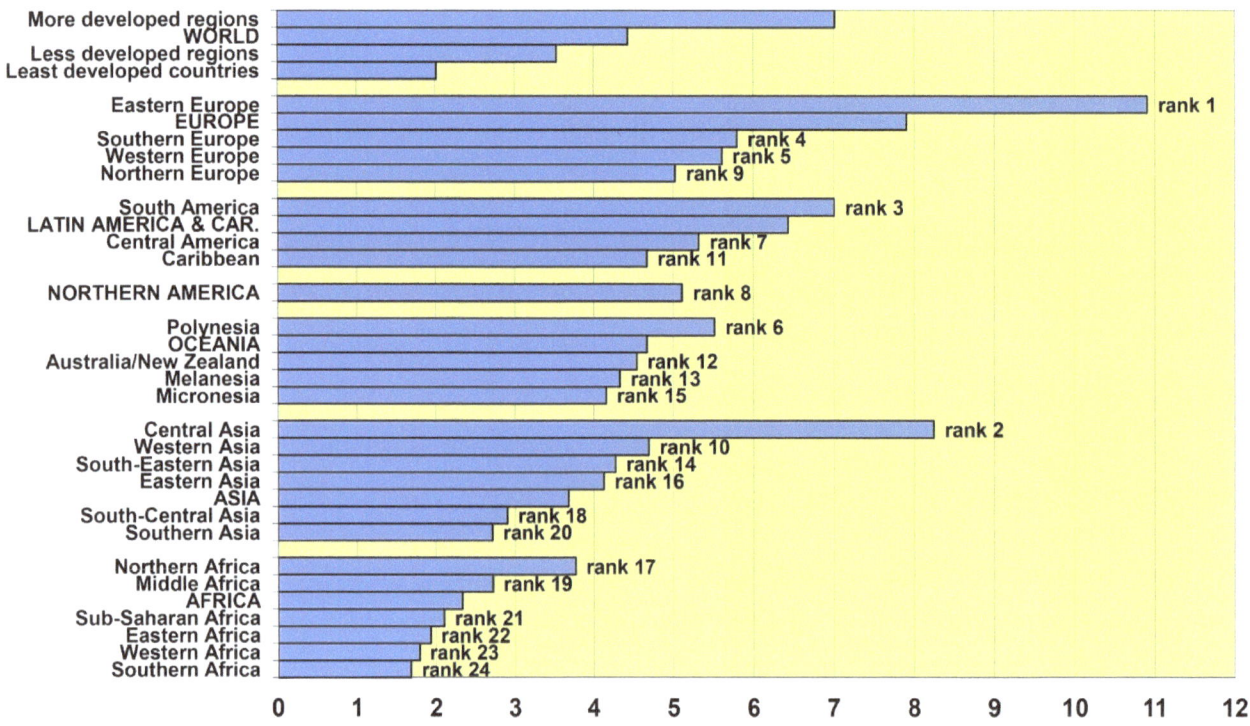

FIGURE 12 Gender disparities in life expectancy at birth for world regions in 2005–2010
SOURCE: Calculation based on data from UN (2011).

On the more detailed disaggregation of world regions the ranks are shown by the magnitude of the gender disparity in life expectancy. By far the highest female-male differences are shown for Eastern Europe and Central Asia; for the former the difference amounts to nearly 11 years and for the latter for more than 8 years, while the world average is more than 4 years. Both of these regions were a part of the political system prevailing in the former Soviet Union and in the associated countries. So for Eastern Europe one of the factors may be the position of women in the society over a long period, the history as well as the life style of men as the ranking of the male life expectancy in countries of Eastern Europe in Table 6 among all 196 countries is much lower than that of female life expectancy.

It is clear that various other factors beyond the level of development affect the magnitude of female over male difference in life expectancy. For cross-section analysis at the country level we have used three variables as indications of the level of development around 2010: rank for GDP per capita (World Bank data from the Human Development Report), rank for the Human Development Index (UNDP, 2011), and rank for life expectancy for females. Over the whole range of 168–196 countries (depending on the available data) there was no significant correlation with the female-male difference in life expectancy with all three indicators.

However, at the both ends of the interval of ranks for female life expectancy as proxy for the level of development there were clear indications that it affects the female-male difference in life expectancy, but not in the middle of the interval. In the group of countries ranking in positions 1–40 there was only one country where the female-male difference in life expectancy was less than 4 years; the unweighted average for this group was 5.4 years. On the other end of the interval, from ranks 157–196 for all countries the female-male difference was below 4 years; on the average the difference was around 2 years, with the exception of Afghanistan all were African countries.

The international ordering by life expectancy at birth might be rather different for females and males. These differences in Table 6 are rather striking for to two groups of countries, one with high negative and one with high positive difference between ranks for females and ranks for males, and a number of countries where this difference in ranks against the international frontier is not so pronounced. This would be hidden if one would calculate ranks for total life expectancy only.

Table 6 shows the results for the two groups of countries for which the difference of female and male rankings is 20 ranks or more, either negative or positive. The extreme negative differences of more than 50 ranks are shown in three Baltic countries, e.g. the rank of Estonia against the international frontier for females was 51, while the corresponding rank for males was 110. On the other extreme of positive differences e.g. the rank for Qatar was 65 for females and only 12 for males. A more complex analysis of various reasons for such extreme difference is needed; including general and specific country factors as these outcomes offer an interesting starting point. The unweighted average of the female-male life expectancy gap of the 21 countries in the first group was 9 years and that for the second group 2.4 years.

In addition to the analysis of the ranks, in the last column in Table 6 the relative posiiton of the countries in the two groups is evaluated by the S-time-distance for female life expectancy against the international frontier of the ten best countries over the period 1950–2010. The average value of S-time-distance behind the international frontier is 32 years for the first group with negative values of difference in ranks (rank females minus rank males), i.e. for the countries where the life expectancy for females ranks much better than that of males. Except for three countries with time distances behind international frontier below 10 years the overall conclusion points to the fact that these countries are not in the top group of the most developed countries compared to the long term trend of Sweden.

This is even more pronounced for the second group with positive values of difference in ranks (rank females minus rank males), i.e. for the countries where the life expectancy for males ranks much better than that of females; the female life expectancy for this group is on the average 46 years behind the international frontier for females. This brief analysis of disparities in the world for female and male life expectancy against the respective benchmarks opens an important background for the earlier discussion of world disparities in life expectancy and female-male disparities.

Country	FEMALES		MALES		Difference between female and male life expectancy (years)	Difference in ranks (rank females minus rank males)	S-time-distance from international frontier for females (in years)
	Life expectancy at birth (years)	Rank Females	Life expectancy at birth (years)	Rank Males			
Estonia	79.17	51	68.35	110	10.8	-59	26
Lithuania	77.24	66	65.46	124	11.8	-58	33
Latvia	77.45	62	66.88	115	10.6	-53	32
Belarus	75.53	94	63.59	135	11.9	-41	41
Hungary	77.64	61	69.54	100	8.1	-39	32
Cape Verde	77.36	64	69.41	102	8.0	-38	33
Russian Federation	74.03	109	61.56	147	12.5	-38	50
Poland	79.85	45	71.17	79	8.7	-34	22
Slovakia	78.65	54	70.73	84	7.9	-30	28
Ukraine	73.54	116	61.78	146	11.8	-30	52
El Salvador	76.08	89	66.55	118	9.5	-29	38
Colombia	76.66	78	69.24	104	7.4	-26	35
Kazakhstan	71.53	127	60.18	152	11.4	-25	(60)
Romania	76.83	73	69.57	98	7.3	-25	35
Argentina	79.07	52	71.53	75	7.5	-23	26
Guadeloupe	82.88	12	75.71	35	7.2	-23	6
Puerto Rico	82.67	19	74.69	42	8.0	-23	7
Bulgaria	76.35	83	69.21	105	7.1	-22	37
Georgia	76.50	81	69.36	103	7.1	-22	36
Republic of Korea	83.25	8	76.48	30	6.8	-22	4
Thailand	77.06	69	70.17	91	6.9	-22	34
Oman	74.83	101	70.88	81	4.0	20	45
Iran (Islamic Rep.)	73.91	110	70.33	89	3.6	21	50
Nepal	68.04	138	66.71	117	1.3	21	(68)
Tunisia	76.04	90	71.89	69	4.2	21	38
Micronesia	69.11	134	67.56	112	1.6	22	(66)
Bangladesh	68.29	136	67.41	113	0.9	23	(67)
China	74.45	104	71.10	80	3.4	24	48
Viet Nam	76.21	86	72.33	62	3.9	24	37
Grenada	76.79	75	73.71	49	3.1	26	35
Occ. Palestinian Ter.	73.81	112	70.60	86	3.2	26	51
Syrian Arab Rep.	76.85	72	73.91	46	2.9	26	35
Belize	76.80	74	73.93	45	2.9	29	35
United Arab Emir.	77.04	70	75.25	40	1.8	30	34
Algeria	73.71	115	70.86	82	2.8	33	51
Jordan	74.29	106	71.65	72	2.6	34	49
Maldives	76.52	80	74.64	43	1.9	37	36
Saudi Arabia	74.41	105	72.24	65	2.2	40	48
Kuwait	75.19	98	73.47	52	1.7	46	43
Bahrain	75.37	96	74.03	44	1.3	52	42
Qatar	77.29	65	78.07	12	-0.8	53	33

TABLE 6 Countries where the differences between female ranks and male ranks were more than 20 ranks in period 2005–2010 and time distances from international frontier for females

NOTE: The values of S-time-distance in the brackets are estimated.

SOURCE: Data from UN (2011) and own calculations based on this data.

Chapter 5

GENDER DISPARITIES IN EU27 COUNTRIES AND NUTS2 REGIONAL LEVEL

Female-male disparity in life expectancy at birth for EU27 countries

Before looking at the gender inequality in life expectancy we show the degree of inequality in female life expectancy between EU27 countries by showing tables of time matrix, S-time-distance, and S-time-step as indicated in the methodology in Chapter 2.

Level	66	67	68	69	70	71	72	73	74	75	76	77	78	79	80	81	82	83	84	85
EU27 females								1964	1970	1974	1979	1983	1988	1994	1999	2003	2006	**2010**		
Inter. frontier								1954	1958	1964	1970	1974	1978	1982	1987	1992	1998	2003	**2008**	
France									1962	1966	1970	1974	1978	1983	1986	1989	1994	2003	2005	**2009**
Spain								1963	1967	1971	1974	1977	1979	1981	1986	1991	1996	2000	2005	**2009**
Italy								1963	1967	1970	1974	1978	1982	1986	1989	1993	1997	2003	2006	**2010**
Portugal	1961	1962	1964	1969	1971	1974	1975	1976	1978	1980	1984	1987	1991	1996	2000	2003	2006	2010	**2011**	
Sweden									1960	1965	1970	1976	1980	1988	1993	2000	**2006**			
Finland								1962	1966	1970	1973	1977	1980	1990	1994	1998	2003	**2006**		
Austria								1964	1972	1976	1979	1984	1987	1990	1995	1999	2004	**2007**		
Cyprus								1973	1975	1976	1978	1980	1986	1992	2000	2005	2006	**2008**		
Luxembourg								1970	1972	1976	1981	1984	1987	1992	1997	2003	2006	**2008**		
Slovenia							1964	1971	1973	1983	1985	1988	1994	1996	2000	2005	2007	**2010**		
Germany							1961	1963	1972	1976	1979	1983	1987	1991	1996	1999	2005	**2010**		
Belgium								1960	1969	1973	1977	1981	1984	1988	1993	2000	2005	**2010**		
Netherlands											1966	1972	1975	1979	1987	2003	2006	**2010**		
Ireland							1961	1967	1973	1979	1982	1987	1991	1999	2001	2003	2006	**2011**		
Greece								1960	1964	1969	1972	1977	1983	1988	1994	2001	2007	**2011**		
UK									1962	1970	1978	1983	1987	1993	1999	2004	2008	**2011**		
Malta						1965	1973	1980	1981	1984	1986	1989	1991	1994	2000	2004	2006	**2011**		
Denmark										1964	1970	1976	1995	1999	2004	**2008**				
Estonia								1994	1995	1996	1999	2002	2005	2007	2009	**2010**				
Czech Rep.								1962	1980	1987	1991	1995	1998	2004	2006	**2011**				
Poland						1963	1965	1967	1972	1984	1994	1997	2000	2004	2008	**2011**				
Slovakia								1965	1975	1985	1992	1998	2004	**2008**						
Lithuania							1961	1962	1964	1995	1996	2006	2008	**2010**						
Hungary						1963	1968	1981	1993	1996	2000	2004	**2007**							
Latvia								1995	1996	1998	2004	2007	**2009**							
Romania			1961	1962	1969	1973	1987	1996	1999	2003	2006	2007	**2011**							
Bulgaria								1963	1969	1997	2000	2003	**2008**							

FIGURE 13 Time matrix for female life expectancy for EU27 countries
SOURCE: Own calculation based on data from Eurostat (2013a); for International frontier UN (2011); for EU27 Eurostat (2006, 2013a).

There is a wealth of information in these tables; very many possible comparisons are not discussed here in detail. While in France, Spain, and Italy the female life expectancy already reached 85 years, in Romania and Bulgaria was around 77 years, a difference of 8 years. The earlier discussion of the female-male differences in life expectancy can be analysed also separately for women and men in terms of time distance lagging behind the international frontier. At a glance one can see that even in the EU27 there are substantial differences in female life expectancy between the member countries.

Comparing the EU27 and international frontier rows in Figures 13 and 14 one can immediately see that international frontier has passed through more levels than EU27 average and that given levels of female life expectancy were attained earlier by the average of the 10 best countries forming international frontier than for EU27 average, which is lagging for about 8 years. The detailed calculation of time distances for EU27 and all individual countries are in Figure 14.

At the level of female life expectancy of 84 years only 3 EU countries, France, Spain, and Italy were ahead of the international frontier average, being 3 years ahead. Fourteen EU countries lagged the international frontier from 3 to 8 years, another 10 countries lagged from 16 years in Denmark to 34 years in Bulgaria.

Level	73	74	75	76	77	78	79	80	81	82	83	84
EU27 females	10	12	10	10	9	10	12	12	11	8	8	
Inter. frontier	0	0	0	0	0	0	0	0	0	0	0	0
France		4	3	1	0	1	1	-1	-3	-4	0	-3
Spain	9	9	7	5	3	1	0	-1	-1	-2	-2	-3
Italy	8	9	7	5	4	5	4	2	1	-1	1	-3
Portugal	22	20	17	14	13	14	14	13	11	8	7	3
Sweden			-3	-5	-4	-2	-2	1	1	2	3	
Finland	8	8	6	4	3	2	8	7	6	5	3	
Austria	9	14	12	10	10	9	8	8	7	6	4	
Cyprus	19	17	13	9	6	8	10	13	13	8	5	
Luxembourg	16	14	13	11	10	10	11	10	11	8	5	
Slovenia	17	15	19	16	14	17	14	13	13	9	7	
Germany	9	14	12	10	9	9	10	9	7	7	7	
Belgium	6	11	9	7	7	6	6	6	8	7	7	
Netherlands				-4	-2	-2	-3	0	11	8	7	
Ireland	13	15	15	12	13	14	18	14	11	8	8	
Greece	6	7	5	3	3	5	6	7	9	9	8	
UK		4	6	9	9	9	12	12	11	10	8	
Malta	26	23	20	17	15	14	12	13	11	8	8	
Denmark			0	1	2	18	17	17	16			
Estonia	40	37	32	30	28	27	26	22	18			
Czech Rep.	8	22	23	22	21	20	22	19	18			
Poland	13	14	20	24	23	22	22	21	18			
Slovakia	11	17	21	22	24	26	26					
Lithuania	8	6	31	27	32	31	29					
Hungary	27	35	32	30	30	30						
Latvia	40	38	35	34	33	31						
Romania	42	41	39	36	33	33						
Bulgaria	15	39	36	34	34							

S-time-distance (in years): (-) time lead, (+) time lag from the benchmark

FIGURE 14 S-time-distance lag in years behind international frontier for females
SOURCE: Own calculation based on Figure 13.

The more detailed estimates of the dynamics used by the S-time-step measure are presented in Figure 15. The values of S-time-step show the number of years needed in the past to reach the next consecutive level of female life expectancy. The average value of S-time-step in the row for EU27 is 4.6 years, i.e. in the past nearly 5 years were needed for increase in 1 year of life expectancy over the analysed period. Portugal shows the highest dynamics from countries with data from 1960.

Level	66	67	68	69	70	71	72	73	74	75	76	77	78	79	80	81	82	83	84	85
EU27 females									6.0	4.0	5.0	4.0	4.7	6.0	5.3	4.3	2.7	4.3		
Inter. frontier									3.6	5.7	5.9	4.5	3.6	4.1	5.2	5.5	5.6	4.7	5.6	
France										4.3	4.3	4.0	4.0	4.6	3.3	3.1	4.2	9.6	2.0	3.8
Spain									3.8	3.8	3.6	2.5	2.0	2.5	4.9	5.1	4.7	4.2	5.1	3.9
Italy									3.8	3.9	4.0	4.0	3.7	3.5	2.9	4.5	3.9	6.2	2.5	4.3
Portugal		0.6	2.2	4.8	2.2	2.3	1.4	1.5	1.8	2.2	3.2	3.0	5.0	4.5	3.6	3.8	2.3	4.5	0.8	
Sweden										4.3	5.0	6.5	4.0	8.0	5.1	6.9	5.5			
Finland									4.0	4.0	3.3	3.3	3.3	10.0	3.6	4.4	5.2	2.7		
Austria									8.0	4.0	3.3	4.5	3.0	3.6	4.6	4.3	4.8	2.8		
Cyprus									1.5	1.5	1.9	1.9	5.8	5.8	7.9	5.6	0.8	2.0		
Luxembourg									1.9	4.5	4.2	3.7	2.8	5.3	4.6	6.1	3.2	1.6		
Slovenia								6.7	2.5	9.7	2.0	3.0	6.3	1.7	4.2	4.9	1.9	2.8		
Germany								2.8	8.3	4.3	3.0	4.0	3.6	4.8	4.2	3.4	6.0	5.0		
Belgium									8.3	4.5	3.7	4.0	3.3	3.5	5.8	6.7	5.3	4.8		
Netherlands													6.0	3.6	3.6	7.6	16.5	3.0	4.0	
Ireland								6.3	6.1	6.0	2.8	4.9	4.7	8.0	1.8	2.2	2.4	4.7		
Greece									4.0	4.6	3.3	4.7	6.0	4.6	6.8	6.6	6.4	3.3		
UK									7.7	8.3	4.5	4.1	6.2	6.0	4.5	4.5	2.6			
Malta							8.0	7.2	1.1	2.5	2.5	2.5	2.5	2.5	6.0	3.8	2.8	4.5		
Denmark											6.4	5.8	19.1	3.7	4.5	4.5				
Estonia									0.7	0.8	3.4	3.0	2.7	2.6	1.4	1.7				
Czech Rep.									17.9	6.5	4.9	3.9	2.3	6.0	2.7	4.2				
Poland							2.0	2.9	4.4	12.2	9.6	3.4	3.0	3.5	4.5	2.8				
Slovakia									9.8	10.0	7.0	6.0	6.0	4.0						
Lithuania								1.3	2.0	30.8	1.4	9.8	2.4	1.9						
Hungary							5.3	13.0	11.8	3.0	3.8	3.9	3.8							
Latvia									0.8	2.8	5.3	3.9	1.6							
Romania				0.8	7.4	3.6	14.0	9.4	2.1	4.5	2.6	1.7	3.3							
Bulgaria									6.7	27.9	2.8	3.3	4.7							

FIGURE 15 S-time-step (years): time needed to achieve the next level of the life expectancy for the females

SOURCE: Own calculation based on Figure 13.

The advantage of women in terms of life expectancy is confirmed for the EU at the country and regional levels. For all EU27 countries the higher life expectancy at birth for women is confirmed for the period for all available data for countries in the period 1960–2011. In Table 7 in 2011 it varied from 3.7 years for the Netherlands to 11.2 years for Lithuania. If we compare the gender disparity with the absolute level of male life expectancy it is shown that it varies from around 5% to 16% of male life expectancy. In other words, for EU27 women are expected to live 7.5% longer than men; in eight countries even more than 10%, in Lithuania even more than 16%.

The method of calculating S-time-distances here is slightly different from that earlier using the time matrix. The level of male life expectancy for 2011 is the starting point, and it is calculated at what time in the time series for females this value has been reached. The differences between the two procedures are small and do not affect the general conclusions. The third column in Table 7 shows the time lag for males behind females for life expectancy at birth. S-time-distance shows a much higher degree of gender disparity than the static measures; the time delay ranges from 16 years to more than 50 years (that female value after 1960 was never as low as the 2011 level of male life expectancy).

What is clear is that there are astonishing differences in gender life expectancy between EU countries. To examine this we calculated ranks separately for females and males against the world list of 196 countries from data in UN (2011) and the respective differences between the two ranks. There are only 12 countries for which the difference in the ranking is lower than 10. In the world context Italy stands out from the EU countries as it is ranked 5 for females and 7 for males, in both cases in the 10 best countries. France is placed at 2 for females, but at 16 for males; Spain showed a similar difference, being placed 6 for females and 21 for males, for Sweden this is reversed, at 11 for females and 6 for males.

Country	Difference between female and male life expectancy (years) in 2011	Gender difference as a percentage of male life expectancy	S-time-distance: Time lag for males behind females in life expectancy	World rank for females 2005-2010	World rank for males 2005-2010	Difference in ranks (females minus males)
Netherlands	3.7	4.7%	30	23	13	10
Cyprus	3.8	4.8%	17	38	25	13
Sweden	3.9	4.9%	26	11	6	5
United Kingdom	4	5.1%	18	31	18	13
Denmark	4.1	5.3%	23	41	32	9
Malta	4.3	5.5%	18	35	31	4
Ireland	4.5	5.7%	16	25	19	6
Greece	4.6	5.9%	26	26	23	3
Germany	4.8	6.1%	23	22	22	0
Italy	5.2	6.5%	22	5	7	-2
Luxembourg	5.1	6.5%	22	29	26	3
Belgium	5.4	6.9%	27	21	24	-3
Austria	5.6	7.2%	24	12	17	-5
Spain	6	7.6%	28	6	21	-15
Portugal	6.4	8.2%	20	30	38	-8
Finland	6.5	8.4%	33	16	33	-17
Czech Republic	6.3	8.4%	25	42	47	-5
Slovenia	6.5	8.5%	23	28	41	-13
France	6.9	8.8%	29	2	16	-14
Bulgaria	7.1	10.0%	> 50	83	105	-22
Romania	7.2	10.1%	38	73	98	-25
Slovakia	7.5	10.4%	> 50	54	84	-30
Hungary	7.5	10.5%	48	61	100	-39
Poland	8.5	11.7%	44	45	79	-34
Estonia	10.1	14.2%	> 50	51	110	-59
Latvia	10.2	14.9%	> 50	62	115	-53
Lithuania	11.2	16.4%	> 50	66	124	-58
EU27	5.8	7.5%	26			

TABLE 7 Female-male disparity in life expectancy at birth for EU27 countries
SOURCE: Own calculation based on data from Eurostat (2006, 2013a); for world ranks UN (2011).

Surprisingly high differences in ranking in Table 7 are found in the last eight countries in the table, indicating that the world ranks for male life expectancy are much worse than that for females. For Estonia, Latvia and Lithuania the difference between the two rankings favour females by more than 50 ranks; e.g. Estonia occupies rank 51 for female and 110 for male life expectancy. The position of women in society over a long period, history and also the lifestyle of men might be influencing these differences in the rankings. A contrasting case is that of the

United Kingdom, where the females ranking is 31 and that of males 18.

Level	60	61	62	63	64	65	66	67	68	69	70	71	72	73	74	75	76	77	78	79	80	81	82	83	84	85
Inter. frontier F														1954	1958	1964	1970	1974	1978	1982	1987	1992	1998	2003	2008	
Inter. frontier M										1955	1964	1973	1977	1982	1987	1992	1997	2001	2004	2009						
EU27 F														1964	1970	1974	1979	1983	1988	1994	1999	2003	2006	2010		
EU27 M								1963	1971	1979	1983	1987	1993	1997	2000	2004	2007	2010								
France F															1962	1966	1970	1974	1978	1983	1986	1989	1994	2003	2005	2009
Spain F														1963	1967	1971	1974	1977	1979	1981	1986	1991	1996	2000	2005	2009
Italy F														1963	1967	1970	1974	1978	1982	1986	1989	1993	1997	2003	2006	2010
Portugal F							1961	1962	1964	1969	1971	1974	1975	1976	1978	1980	1984	1987	1991	1996	2000	2003	2006	2010	2011	
Sweden F															1960	1965	1970	1976	1980	1988	1993	2000	2006			
Finland F														1962	1966	1970	1973	1977	1980	1990	1994	1998	2003	2006		
Austria F														1964	1972	1976	1979	1984	1987	1990	1995	1999	2004	2007		
Cyprus F														1973	1975	1976	1978	1980	1986	1992	2000	2005	2006	2008		
Luxembourg F														1970	1972	1976	1981	1984	1987	1992	1997	2003	2006	2008		
Slovenia F													1964	1971	1973	1983	1985	1988	1994	1996	2000	2005	2007	2010		
Germany F													1961	1963	1972	1976	1979	1983	1987	1991	1996	1999	2005	2010		
Belgium F														1960	1969	1973	1977	1981	1984	1988	1993	2000	2005	2010		
Netherlands F															1966	1972	1975	1979	1987	2003	2006	2010				
Ireland F													1961	1967	1973	1979	1982	1987	1991	1999	2001	2003	2006	2011		
Greece F														1960	1964	1969	1972	1977	1983	1988	1994	2001	2007	2011		
United Kingdom F															1962	1970	1978	1983	1987	1993	1999	2004	2008	2011		
Malta F												1965	1973	1980	1981	1984	1986	1989	1991	1994	2000	2004	2006	2011		
Denmark F															1964	1970	1976	1995	1999	2004	2008					
Estonia F														1994	1995	1996	1999	2002	2005	2007	2009	2010				
Czech Republic F														1962	1980	1987	1991	1995	1998	2004	2006	2011				
Poland F												1963	1965	1967	1972	1984	1994	1997	2000	2004	2008	2011				
Italy M								1964	1970	1976	1981	1984		1987	1992	1995	1998	2001	2005	2008	2011					
Sweden M													1972	1981	1986	1991	1994	1999	2003	2007						
Slovakia F														1965	1975	1985	1992	1998	2004	2008						
Cyprus M										1973	1975	1977		1982	1989	1998	2001	2005	2007	2010						
Spain M									1963	1969	1973	1977	1979	1983	1993	1997	2000	2004	2007	2010						
Netherlands M												1972	1977	1984	1993	1997	2002	2004	2007	2010						
Lithuania F													1961	1962	1964	1995	1996	2006	2008	2010						
Malta M								1963	1980	1981	1983	1986	1988	1991	1993	1998	2000	2006	2009	2010						
United Kingdom M									1961	1972	1979	1983	1986	1991	1995	1999	2002	2005	2008	2011						
Hungary F												1963	1968	1981	1993	1996	2000	2004	2007							
France M								1961	1967	1973	1979	1984	1987	1991	1995	1999	2003	2005	2009							
Latvia F														1995	1996	1998	2004	2007	2009							
Ireland M										1973	1980	1986	1990	1996	2000	2002	2003	2005	2009							
Greece M									1960	1961	1964	1969	1973	1980	1987	1996	2001	2006	2009							
Germany M								1961	1973	1977	1981	1984	1990	1994	1997	2000	2003	2006	2010							
Luxembourg M									1974	1977	1982	1985	1988	1992	1995	1998	2003	2004	2007	2010						
Austria M								1972	1976	1980	1984	1986	1989	1994	1997	1999	2003	2006	2010							
Romania F									1961	1962	1969	1973	1987	1996	1999	2003	2006	2007	2011							
Bulgaria F													1963	1969	1997	2000	2003	2008								
Belgium M								1960	1971	1976	1980	1984	1987	1993	1996	2002	2004	2008								
Denmark M													1976	1989	1996	1998	2003	2005	2009							
Finland M							1965	1972	1976	1979	1982	1990	1993	1996	2000	2003	2007	2010								
Portugal M	1961	1962	1966	1969	1971	1976	1977	1978	1980	1983	1986	1993	1997	2000	2003	2005	2007	2010								
Slovenia M						1970	1972	1983	1985	1988	1994	1996	2000	2004	2005	2007	2009									
Czech Republic M							1969	1980	1991	1993	1995	1998	2003	2005	2008											
Poland M					1963	1991	1993	1996	1999	2001	2007	2010														
Slovakia M							1991	1993	1999	2003	2008	2011														
Hungary M						1994	1996	1999	2001	2006	2008	2011														
Estonia M		1994	1995	1996	1998	2002	2003	2005	2008	2008	2009	2011														
Romania M						1962	1998	1999	2004	2006	2010	2011														
Bulgaria M								1997	1999	2005	2009															
Latvia M	1995	1995	1996	1996	1998	2002	2007	2008	2009																	
Lithuania M				1995	1996	2007	2008	2009	2010																	

Females   Males

FIGURE 16 Time matrix containing both female (F) and male (M) life expectances for EU countries

NOTE: International frontier F (females) and international frontier M (males) represent the unweighted average of the best 10 countries in the world for life expectancy for each five-years average in UN (2011) for the respective gender.
SOURCE: Own calculation based on data from Eurostat (2006, 2013a); for International frontier UN (2011).

Figure 16 presents a large time matrix combining female and male life expectancy for all EU27 countries over the analysed period. It is a clear visualisation over many units and over time that offers a condensed summary at a glance. This time matrix condenses information of combined tables of time series of female and male life expectancy for the period of more than 50 years (1960-2011), which in the Eurostat extended database amounts to more than 2500 entries; in this time matrix it is condensed to much smaller number of entries (less than 600). This presents a first level visualisation that usefully complements the details in the original database by showing the easily understandable summary overview.

Overall it is easy to observe that the female time series have reached much higher values than that for males. Women life expectancy is higher than that of males in all EU countries (easily observed if we would arrange the rows as for EU27 F and EU27 M). This tendency is so strong that the first 21 positions in Figure 16 ordered by the value of life expectancy are that of female life expectancy. Only in six countries (Slovakia, Lithuania, Hungary, Latvia, Romania, and Bulgaria) the female life expectancy was mixed with the male life expectancy among some above average EU countries.

This large combined time matrix enables comparisons across gender within a group as well as comparisons of levels of either female or male life expectancy between different units used in the figure. The choice between these possibilities depends on the analytical priority of the user.

If one would be concerned predominantly with gender differences within countries the arrangement in the upper part for EU27 averages for female and male values (or between the values for the international frontier) would be easier to observe gender disparities directly. Only for the span of life expectancy between 73 and 77 years values for both genders are available, and for these values the rounded S-time-distances amount accordingly to 33, 30, 30, 28, and 27 years of lag of male life expectancy behind female life expectancy (i.e. so many years earlier have these levels for males been achieved by females).

The time matrix format with the table-graph characteristics allows at the same time two types of comparisons between countries and genders and calculation of corresponding differences between countries and genders. First, visually one can observe which approximate levels were achieved over the period as well as the dynamics in terms of the number of steps in life expectancy achieved (depending on the data available). Second, from the values of times in the time matrix further measures can be calculated, i.e. S-time-distances between genders and countries, on the one hand, and S-time-steps as additional measure of dynamics, on the other. Out of a very large number of possible comparisons in Figure 16 only a small number of available comparisons can be commented here.

Figure 17 shows the results of S-time-distance delays of male life expectancy behind female life expectancy over the analysed period. The general conclusion is that the time distance perspective indicates that in the past the gender difference in life expectancy in the EU has been very large and rather stable.

Both for the averages for the international frontier and for the EU27 average it is shown that the time delay was at about 27 years; the relationship is very persistent and it changes very slowly. Broadly speaking, at the lower end of the table there are 10 countries with S-time-distance delay of more than 30 years, for five of them (Estonia, Slovakia, Lithuania, Latvia, and Bulgaria) there was no possibility to calculate the delay. For these five countries we can estimate that the time delay of male behind the female life expectancy is more than 50 years, i.e. more than half a century.

Level	66	67	68	69	70	71	72	73	74	75	76	77	78	79	80
Inter. frontier M								28	29	29	27	27	27	27	
EU27 M								33	30	30	28	27			
France M									33	32	33	31	31		
Spain M								20	26	26	26	27	28	28	
Italy M								24	25	25	24	22	23	22	22
Portugal M	15	16	16	14	15	20	22	23	24	25	24	24			
Sweden M										31	29	29	27	27	
Finland M								34	34	33	34	34			
Austria M								30	25	24	24	22	24		
Cyprus M								9	14	22	22	25	21	18	
Luxembourg M								25	27	27	23	23	23		
Slovenia M						35		33	32	24	24				
Germany M						30		30	25	24	24	23	23		
Belgium M								33	28	29	27	28			
Netherlands M											36	33	31	31	
Ireland M							29	29	27	23	22	18	18		
Greece M								20	23	27	29	29	26		
United Kingdom M									33	29	24	22	21	18	
Malta M						21	15	11	12	15	14	17	18	17	
Denmark M										39	35	33			
Estonia M															
Czech Republic M								43	28						
Poland M						45	45								
Slovakia M															
Lithuania M															
Hungary M						48									
Latvia M															
Romania M		42	44	40		38									
Bulgaria M															

FIGURE 17 S-time-distance (years): time lag for males (M) behind females in life expectancy
SOURCE: Own calculation based on data from Figure 16.

This may be in some instances a question of shorter time series but this does not in any way change the overall conclusion that the time distance method significantly showed the large time distance perspective of the degree of disparity between female and male life expectancy that is not taken into account in the standard static analysis of disparities.

A more detailed analysis for reasons is very complex and requires a large systematic research project dealing with both medical and social factors. One line of factors contributing to such dominant statistical fact of higher female than male life expectancy is possible difference in our genes. An example of such studies is that looking at the tendency for females to outlive males in different species in the animal kingdom (Monash University, 2012). In addition to economic and social factors there are important differences in life style and time use.

In analysing the gender differences in life expectancy between the EU27 countries some obvious possible explanatory factors like Global Gender Gap index of World Economic Forum (Hausmann, Tyson, and Zahidi, 2011), women's voting rights (UNDP, 2007), or real adjusted gross disposable income of households per capita (Eurostat, 2012c) did not show high degree of association.

Gender disparities for 269 NUTS2 EU27 regions

Disparities in life expectancy in the EU27 can be analysed also at the regional level. Figure 18 presents values of S-time-distances for NUTS2 regions in 2010, compared to the time when such level was attained in the trend of the average for international frontier. Of the 269 NUTS2 regions one half of them are lagging 7.3 years or more behind the female international frontier. It is interesting to see that at this lower level of the aggregation from 55 NUTS2 regions which were in 2010 showing time lead against the average of international frontier; 51 of these regions were from the three countries being ahead in Figure 14 (France, Spain, and Italy), the rest were two regions from Austria, and one from Greece and Finland.

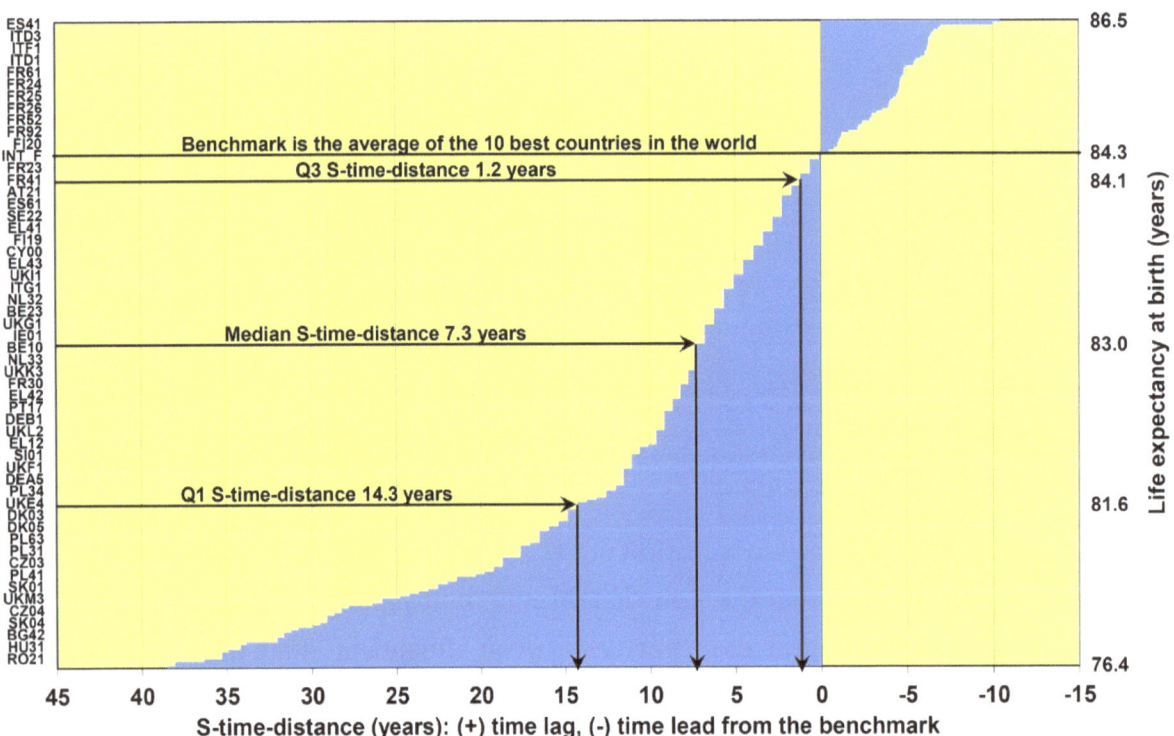

FIGURE 18 Values of female life expectancy for NUTS2 regions in 2010 compared to the time when such level was attained in the average trend for 10 best countries in the world

NOTE: Because of the high number of regions included, on the vertical axis only every fifth region code is shown.
SOURCE: Calculation based on data Eurostat (2012b); for International frontier UN (2011).

Looking at the gender disparities in life expectancy at the regional level conclusions were drawn when data were also analysed for 2010 for NUTS1 and NUTS2 regional levels in Table 5.

For the first, gender disparity in life expectancy ranged from 3.8 to 10.9 years, and the median value was 5.9 years; for the second it ranged from 2.3 to 10.9 years of life, with a median value of 5.5 years. The median value for 3118 US counties for female-male disparity in 2007 was also 5.5 years. The results for 2007 showed that in all of the 3118 US counties, female life expectancy was higher than that of male life expectancy (Kulkarni et al., 2011).

LEXP level	67	68	69	70	71	72	73	74	75	76	77	78	79	80	81	82	83	84	85	86	87
Spain										1	2	4	8	3	1	1	1	5	6	5	1
Italy												2	9	9	1		2	4	12	3	
France								1	2	4	7	9	2	1	1	1	3	10	10	1	
Greece										1		10		2	1	5	5	1	1		
Finland							1			1	2				1		4		1		
Austria										1	4	2	2			1	4	4			
Germany									1	6	11	12	7			20	15	2			
United Kingdom F													1	2	9	9	14	2			
United Kingdom M									1	3	9	7	8	9							
Slovenia									1		1					1		1			
Belgium								1	2	1	1	4	2		2	2	6	1			
Sweden												1	7			1	6	1			
Netherlands											1	5	6			5	7				
Portugal					1	1				2	3	1	1		1	1	3				
Ireland													2				2				
Cyprus													1				1				
Luxembourg											1						1				
Malta													1				1				
Czech Republic						2		2	3	1			1	3	3	1					
Denmark										2	2	1		1	3	1					
Poland				1	8	3	4							2	7	6	1				
Estonia					1									1							
Slovakia					2	1	1						1	2	1						
Hungary		1	1	3	1	1						1	5	1							
Romania			4	3		1				1	5	1	1								
Bulgaria			3	2	1					3	1	2									
Latvia		1											1								
Lithuania	1												1								

Females | Males

FIGURE 19 Frequency distribution of number of NUTS2 regions in 2010 by levels of life expectancy
SOURCE: Own calculation based on data from Eurostat (2012b).

Figure 19 shows the frequency distribution of the number of NUTS2 regions in 2010 by the levels of life expectancy by country and gender. Also at the regional level it is remarkable that in no country the highest level for males would be higher or equal to the lowest level for females (with the exception of the United Kingdom, for which we therefore introduced two separate rows for genders). But for the UK, too, in all NUTS2 regions the female life expectancy was higher than that of males.

In this figure the overwhelming higher positions of female over male levels of life expectancy is even stronger than it was in Figure 16 dealing with the country levels for the EU27. It is especially pronounced for the last seven countries in Figure 19, which were also among the countries with the highest values of S-time-distance lag of males behind females in Figure 17.

Regional results for UK and Italy

For a smaller number of EU27 countries we can undertake more detailed analysis, in this case for the UK and Italy. Figure 20 shows the situation at the NUTS2 level in the UK as the example of an individual country. For the UK the female life expectancy at the level of 82 years was about 10 years behind the international frontier. When we estimate S-time-distances for 37 NUTS2 regions, all of them fell behind the international frontier for females, the lag ranged from 0.4 years for Surrey, East and West Sussex to 25 years for South Western Scotland.

Level of life expectancy (years)	S-time-distance (years) of time delay of UK NUTS2 regions behind the international frontier of females							S-time-distance (years) of time delay of UK NUTS2 regions behind the international frontier of males								
	78	79	80	81	82	83	84	72	73	74	75	76	77	78	79	80
International frontier	0	0	0	0	0	0	0	0	0	0	0	0	0	0		
EU27 average	10	12	12	11	8	8		16	14	13	11	10	9			
UK		11	12	11	10						8	7	5	4	4	
Surrey, East and West Sussex				1	3	3	0					-3	-2	-1		
Dorset and Somerset				1	2	2	1					-4	-4	-1		
Berkshire, Buckinghamshire and Oxfordshire				7	6	3	1					-3	-1	-1		
Devon				2	5	3						-1	0	0		
Hampshire and Isle of Wight			6	7	5	3						1	0	0	-1	
East Anglia				5	5	3						-2	0	-1		
Outer London			6	8	6	4					2	2	2	1		
North Yorkshire			7	8	5	5					1	0	-1	0		
Gloucestershire, Wiltshire and Bristol/Bath area				7	6	5						-3	-1	-1		
Highlands and Islands				10	6	6						4	4	4		
Essex			7	8	6	6					1	0	0	0		
Inner London		13	13	11	8	6		17	14	12	10	7	5	4		
Herefordshire, Worcestershire and Warwickshire				7	8	7	6				1	1	0	1		
Bedfordshire and Hertfordshire			6	9	7	6					1	-1	0	0		
Cornwall and Isles of Scilly			6	6	6	6					1	0	0	-1		
Kent			7	11	8						1	2	3	1		
Leicestershire, Rutland and Northamptonshire			10	11	8						2	3	3	2		
East Wales		11	11	11	9					6	7	5	4	4		
Lincolnshire			12	11	10						4	3	4	2		
Shropshire and Staffordshire		12	13	12	10					7	6	6	5	5		
Cheshire (NUTS 2006)		11	12	11	11					6	5	3	4	3		
Cumbria		11	12	11	11					8	7	4	4	4		
Derbyshire and Nottinghamshire		12	12	12	11					6	7	6	3	4		
West Midlands		12	16	14	11				11	12	11	9	8			
Northern Ireland (UK)		14	13	11					11	9	7	5	8			
West Wales and The Valleys		11	15	13							8	8	7	8		
East Yorkshire and Northern Lincolnshire			13	14							6	7	6	8		
West Yorkshire		13	15	15							9	10	7	8		
South Yorkshire		12	16	16					11	9	8	7	8			
Northumberland and Tyne and Wear	16	18	17	16					12	12	10	8	8			
Lancashire		15	17	16					11	12	10	8				
Tees Valley and Durham	16	18	18	16					12	11	9	8	8			
Eastern Scotland			18	16								11	9			
Greater Manchester	16	18	19	17					14	13	12	11				
Merseyside (NUTS 2006)	16	21	21	17					17	14	13	11				
North Eastern Scotland		23	22									17	15			
South Western Scotland	25	25								21	21					

S-time-distance (in years): (-) time lead, (+) time lag from the benchmark

FIGURE 20 How does female and male life expectancy in UK regions compare with the international frontier of 10 best countries for female and male life expectancy in the world?
SOURCE: Own calculation based on data Eurostat (2012b); for International frontier own calculations based on data from UN (2011).

When calculating the same S-time-distance measure from the international frontier for males several NUTS2 regions in the UK were ahead of the international frontier. The UK average for males was 4 years behind the respective international frontier, while at the NUTS2 level at the level of 78 years about 14 regions were at about, or one year ahead or behind the international frontier. The empty fields for level 79 indicate that in these regions in the UK for males were at level that was not yet achieved as the average of the frontier. The difference in the position of UK regions for female and male life expectancy against the international frontier might be an important factor to investigate why the UK is in Table 7 the country in the EU27 with one of the smallest female-male difference in life expectancy.

Level of life expectancy (years)	S-time-distance (years) of time delay of Italian NUTS2 regions behind the international frontier of females							S-time-distance (years) of time delay of Italian NUTS2 regions behind the international frontier of males								
	79	80	81	82	83	84	85	72	73	74	75	76	77	78	79	80
International frontier	0	0	0	0	0	0		0	0	0	0	0	0	0		
EU27 average	12	12	11	8	8			16	14	13	11	10	9			
Marche (NUTS 2006)			-2	-6	-7	-8						-5	-4	-5	-5	
Provincia Autonoma Trento (NUTS 2006)			-1	-6	-7	-5			8	5	3	2	1	-1	-2	
Provincia Autonoma Bolzano/Bozen (NUTS 2006)			-2	-5	-5	-5			8	4	2	0	-1	-1	-3	
Toscana (NUTS 2006)			-1	-4	-5	-5					-1	-2	-3	-3	-5	
Veneto (NUTS 2006)			-1	-4	-5	-5				5	3	1	-1	-1	-3	
Molise			0	0	-3	-4					-1	-2	0	1	-1	
Umbria (NUTS 2006)			-1	-4	-4	-7					-1	-2	-2	-3	-3	
Abruzzo			-1	-3	-4	-5					-1	-2	-2	-2	-3	
Emilia-Romagna (NUTS 2006)			-1	-4	-4	-5				3	0	-1	-2	-1	-4	
Lombardia		4	0	-2	-3	-3			9	7	4	2	1	0	-2	
Sardegna		3	1	-3	0	-3				4	3	2	3	1	-1	
Friuli-Venezia Giulia (NUTS 2006)		3	0	-1	-2	-3			9	6	4	2	3	1	-1	
Basilicata		5	3	1	-2	-2					-1	-1	-2	-1	-2	
Liguria		4	1	-2	1	-2			8	4	4	1	1	0	-1	
Lazio (NUTS 2006)		4	1	0	1	-2				4	2	1	1	1	-1	
Piemonte		4	2	1	1	-2				5	4	2	3	1	-1	
Calabria		5	2	1	1	-1					0	0	-2	-1	-1	
Puglia		4	1	0	0	-1					0	-2	-2	-1	-2	
Valle d'Aosta/Vallée d'Aoste		4	-1	0	1	-1		15	12	10	8	6	5	3		
Sicilia	10	8	6	5	4					4	2	1	0	1		
Campania	10	9	8	6	5			10	8	7	6	5				

S-time-distance (in years): (-) time lead, (+) time lag from the benchmark

FIGURE 21 How does female and male life expectancy in Italian regions compare with the international frontier of 10 best countries for female and male life expectancy in the world?
SOURCE: Own calculation based on data Eurostat (2012b); for International frontier own calculations based on data from UN (2011).

The situation in Italy is different from that in the UK in two respects. Firstly, Italy is ahead of the international frontiers for both females and males. In both instances all Italian regions were ahead of the international frontiers, with the exception of two regions for females and three regions for males. Also, at the level of 85 years of female life expectancy 8 regions were already at level that has not yet been achieved for the average of international frontier; for males this was the case only for one region at the level of 80 years of male life expectancy.

Secondly, for females the S-time-distance shows that they were more years ahead of the respective international frontier than males. This is opposite to the situation in the UK where the situation for males was closer to the international frontier.

Sicherl (2013b) calculated static percentage and time distance deviations in 2008 for gender values of NUTS2 Italian regions from the trend of country average of total life expectancy. It was clear that all values of female life expectancy are higher and ahead of total life expectancy, and that the static percentage differences ranging from -5% for males to 5% for females showed a much smaller deviation from the average than S-time-distances, which ranged from about -15 years of time lead for females to about 15 years of time lag for males behind the trend of the average life expectancy of the country. The hypothesis that empirically the degree of disparity may be very different in static terms and in time distance was strongly confirmed in the case of Italy as an example regarding regions in individual countries.

Chapter 6

CONCLUSIONS

1. The results show nearly unanimous conclusion that female life expectancy at birth is higher than that for males, this holds for countries including 99.5% of the world population. These statistical results bring food for thought for further analysis of the situation that the gender disparity in life expectancy is so much in favour of women and thus standing out against so many domains where the gender disparity is in many countries leaning in the other direction.

The UN World Population Prospects (The 2010 Revision) for the period 1950–2010 illustrate that in the interval 2005–2010 the difference in favour of women was ranging from about 2 years for the least developed countries to about 7 years for the more developed regions (MDR) of the world. For the MDR female-male difference in life expectancy at birth would by 2100 come to more than 5 years and to more than 4 years for other aggregates. Without major changes in health conditions the UN estimates expect that higher female than male life expectancy at birth would prevail over the whole period of 150 years.

2. The conclusion that the gender disparity in life expectancy is very persuasive and a long-standing phenomenon is further confirmed by introducing the time distance statistical measure as another complementary perception of the degree of the female-male disparity in life expectancy. In graphical terms, the usual way to compare time-series is to look at the *vertical* dimension, i.e. for a given point in time. The S-time-distance approach provides an additional perspective, comparing time-series in the *horizontal* dimension, i.e. for a given level of the variable it looks at the difference in time when the compared units reached the same selected level of the indicator.

3. Empirically, the degree of disparity may be very different in static terms and in time distance, which leads to new conclusions and semantics important for policy considerations. This innovation opens the possibility for simultaneous two-dimensional comparisons of time series data in two specified dimensions: vertically (standard measures of static difference) as well as horizontally (Sicherl time distance), providing a new dimension of analysis to a variety of problems. They can give different perceptions of the order of magnitude of inequality within and between countries, as both dimensions matter. The time distance methodology is explained in Chapter 2 with further sources in the Appendix.

4. Such a broader concept of the overall degree of disparity can lead to a different perception of the extent of disparity than the conventional static measures alone. Comparing disparity in the overall life expectancy for the countries between China and Sweden the static difference against Sweden was less than 10 percent for China (which may appear to be small) while the S-time-distance was 51 years (which gives a very different perception of the magnitude of the gap). The approach is universal, understandable, and applicable to a wide variety of fields at both the macro and micro levels. Since time distance view provides an additional dimension of temporal disparity, results by other methods are left unchanged but new conclusions can be reached.

5. As a background to the analysis of gender disparity in life expectancy Chapter 3 examined the world inequality in life expectancy and infant mortality across countries. S-time-distance in years against the long-term trends of Sweden as benchmark were calculated for the 2005–2010 level of female and male life expectancy at birth in each of the 196 countries. For females median value of S-time-distance lag behind Sweden amounted to 46 years, which means that about 98 countries lagged Sweden by more than that; 20 countries even more than 110 years. For males median value of S-time-distance lag behind Sweden amounted to 58 years, for 18 countries even more than 110 years. The static difference was 9.2 years, percentage difference about 12 percent, and time distance for the median for males more than half a century. Time distance lens brings additional perception of the magnitude and persistence of the world disparities in this indicator, both for males and females.

6. Another set of results for the analysis of disparities in life expectancy in the world between countries separately for men and for women, measured both by static measures and S-time-distance, to build a multidimensional perception of the degree of disparities with three statistical measures between the international frontier (defined as the best ten countries for female and male life expectancy) and the world average for the period 2005–2010 shows:

- for females the absolute difference shows that the international frontier is around 14 years higher than the world average, in percentage terms about 16 percent higher, and in time distance measure the world average is more than 55 years behind the international frontier;
- for males the absolute difference is around 13 years, in percentage terms about 17 percent, and in time distance the world average is more than 55 years behind the international frontier.

This brings an additional perspective of the much larger magnitude and persistence of world disparities beyond that of the static perspective.

7. Chapter 4 examines the dispersion of female-male differences in life expectancy at birth in two dimensions: the cross-section of countries at a given point in time, and the gap in time when the same levels of life expectancy were achieved by females and by males. The static analysis for 2005–2010 shows that the unweighted average for 196 countries the female-male differences in life expectancy amounted to 4.6 years, with standard deviation of 2.56 years. Out of the 95% confidence interval dropped five countries with negative female-male differences at the lower end and seven countries with the female-male difference over 10 years at the higher end.

Table 5 shows static measures of gender disparities in life expectancy for five levels of analysis: at the world level 196 countries for 2005–2010, EU27 countries together with 97 NUTS1 and 269 NUTS2 regions around 2010, and 3118 USA counties in 2007. In all EU27 countries and regions as well as in all USA counties there was the same conclusion that female life expectancy was higher than that for males.

8. S-time-distance for the world average, i.e. the horizontal gap between trends of female and male life expectancy amounted to 20 years. This means that the male life expectancy in the 2005–2010 period was achieved by females already in the period 1985–1990. S-time-distance between levels of male life expectancy in 2008 and the trends of female values was 28 years for the EU27 and 35 years for the USA. The low growth rate of life expectancy indicates that this gender disparity will be very difficult to eliminate.

9. One of the main points in this study: the astonishing differences between countries for gender inequality in life expectancy are shown by comparing the respective world ranks in Table 6. There are two groups of about 20 countries each, which show great differences in the ranks (these differences range from 20 to 50 ranks in both directions) for females and males in the respective standings in the world. In one group the life expectancy for females ranks much better than that of males, in the other group males rank much higher than females. If one would rank countries in life expectancy only by total life expectancy these important differences would be suppressed.

10. The extreme negative differences of more than 50 ranks are shown in three Baltic countries, e.g. the rank of Estonia against the international frontier for females was 51, while the corresponding rank for males was 110. On the other extreme of differences with algebraically positive values, e.g. the rank for Qatar was 65 for females and only 12 for males. The unweighted average of the female-male life expectancy gap of the 21 countries in the first group was 9 years and that for the second group 2.4 years. It is of interest to notice that these two groups of about 20 countries with the highest differences in female-male disparity in either direction are not positioned at very high general level of development.

11. For a smaller number of EU27 countries we can undertake more detailed analysis in Chapter 5. Such analysis of the gaps behind the international frontier is presented for the EU27 countries showing the time matrix as an innovative complementary approach for looking at time-series data. It is defined for selected levels of a given variable and shows in which year various units (countries, regions, etc.) achieved these levels. The time matrix provides a good summary overview over many units and years and also a first-level visualisation tool. Beyond that, time matrix enables one way of estimating two statistical measures, S-time-distance and S-time-step, outlined in the methodological section. A large time matrix combining female and male life expectancy for all EU27 countries over the analysed period in Figure 16 is an outstanding example of clear visualisation over many units and over time that offers a condensed summary at a glance. This time matrix condenses information of combined tables of time series of female and male life expectancy for the period of more than 50 years (1960-2011), which in the Eurostat extended database amounts to more than 2500 entries; in this time matrix it is condensed to much smaller number of entries (less than 600). This presents a first level visualisation that usefully complements the details in the original database by showing the easily understandable summary dynamic overview.

12. The advantage of women in terms of life expectancy is confirmed for the EU at the country and regional levels. In 2011 the absolute difference varied from 3.7 years for the Netherlands to 11.2 years for Lithuania; in percentage terms it varies from around 5% to 16% of male life expectancy. In other words, for EU27 average women are expected to live 7.5% longer than men; in eight countries even more than 10%, in Lithuania even more than 16%.

13. Both for the averages for the international frontier and for the EU27 average it is shown that the time delay for life expectancy of males behind females was at about 27 years; the relationship is very persistent and it changes very slowly. Broadly speaking, at the lower end of Figure 17 there are 10 countries with S-time-distance delay of more than 30 years, for five of them (Estonia, Slovakia, Lithuania, Latvia and Bulgaria) there was no possibility to calculate the delay. For these five countries we can estimate that the time delay of male behind the female life expectancy is more than 50 years, i.e. more than half a century.

14. Looking at the level of female life expectancy, out of the 269 NUTS2 regions one half of them were lagging 7.3 years or more behind the international frontier for women. Looking at absolute differences in gender disparity in life expectancy for these EU27 NUTS2 regions ranged from 2.3 to 10.9 years of life, with a median value of 5.5 years; the median value for 3118 US counties for female-male disparity in 2007 was also 5.5 years (for all EU27 regions and US counties female life expectancy was higher than that of male life expectancy).

15. An interesting example is that of the female life expectancy for 37 NUTS2 regions in the United Kingdom. The time gaps for individual UK regions behind the international frontier range for females from a few months for the best region to 25 years for South Western Scotland. Contrary to that, for males several NUTS2 regions in the UK were ahead of the international frontier. The situation for Italian regions is different from that in the UK in two respects. Firstly, most of the Italian regions are ahead of the international frontiers for both females and males. Secondly, for females the S-time-distance shows that they were more years ahead of the respective international frontier than males.

16. Two major conclusions, that female life expectancy at birth is higher than that for males for 99.5 percent of the world population, on the one hand, and that there is a astonishing great dispersion of this gender difference among countries, on the other, have been clearly established. Future multifaceted research will have to address two sets of questions in this respect.

17. The first important question for the long-run is the common set of factors influencing that the gender disparity in life expectancy is so overwhelming in favour of women around the globe. At this stage only few hypotheses to be studied can be mentioned. One obvious factor to look at is the genes. Another factor relates to their motherhood role, actual and potential, both to the medical and emotional consequences. In addition to their other roles in the society women are very much concerned with the domestic care of the family, which is shown also by the time use patterns. Thus in daily life they can see their results and usefulness in this domain continuously and the fulfilment in this area might also contribute to longer life span. Needless to say, it is a very complex question but the statistical facts are clear.

18. The second issue is the astonishingly great dispersion of this gender difference among countries, which poses a set of questions that are superimposed on the first set of questions above. These differential conditions between countries are very important for understanding of special conditions and policy actions to be taken in different countries. This set of factors is much more varied (level of development, position of women in the society and political system, gender disparities in other domains, differences in income, wealth and ownership arrangements, personal and family relationships, access to many resources, capacity and use of human resources, life style and time use, etc.).

For the second group we can here mention only two features which were analysed to a certain extend. In comparison between MDR and LDR it was seen that at the lower level of development it is in general considerably more difficult to come to higher statistical values of gender disparity. However, when looking at more detailed situation at comparable levels of development it was established that other factors were more important in determining the differences in gender disparity. It was seen that by far the highest female-male differences are shown for Eastern Europe and Central Asia; regions that were a part of the political system prevailing in the former Soviet Union and in the associated countries, so the history and life styles need to be studied to explain this. A more complex analysis of various reasons for these and other differences is needed, including general and specific country factors; these outcomes offer an interesting starting point.

19. The statistical analysis clearly established significant differences in life expectancy at birth between genders, on the one hand, and striking differences between countries and regions, on the other. The reasons for such great dispersions of the analysed indicators are multifaceted and varied, they are important for explaining the present situation in individual countries and groups of countries. However, there is also the importance of the common factors in the first group for better understanding of the gender disparity in this domain. All these factors are very complex and interconnected; they include medical, social, and economic factors requiring large systematic research project(s).

REFERENCES

Eurostat (2006), Life expectancy by sex and age [mlexpec]. Accessed January 3, 2006.

Eurostat (2012a), Life table, LIFEXP - Life expectancy at given exact age (ex).

Eurostat (2012b), Life expectancy at given exact age (ex) by NUTS 2 regions. Accessed July 6, 2012 (for females);accessed January 19, 2013 (for males).

Eurostat (2012c), Real adjusted gross disposable income of households per capita.

Eurostat (2013a), Life expectancy by age and sex [demo_mlexpec]. Accessed July 22, 2013.

Eurostat (2013b), Infant mortality rates.

Granger, C.W.J. and Jeon, Y. (1997), "Measuring Lag Structure in Forecasting Models - The Introduction of Time Distance," *Discussion Paper* 97-24. University of California, San Diego.

Hausmann, R., Tyson, L.D., Zahidi, S. (2011), *The Global Gender Gap Report 2011*. World Economic Forum, Geneva, Switzerland.

Hosseinpoor, A.R. et al. (2012), "International shortfall inequality in life expectancy in women and in men, 1950–2010," *Bulletin of the World Health Organization*; Type: Research, Article ID: BLT.11.097378.

Human Mortality Database (2006), University of California, Berkeley (USA), and Max Planck Institute for Demographic Research (Germany), www.mortality.org. Accessed August 10 2007.

IHME (2011), "Life expectancy in most US counties falls behind world's healthiest nations," News Release. June 15.

ITU (2010), *Measuring the Information Society 2010*. Geneva.

Kulkarni et al. (2011), "Falling behind: life expectancy in US counties from 2000 to 2007 in an international context," *Population Health Metrics* 2011 9:16, doi:10.1186/1478-7954-9-16.

Maddison, A. (2010), *Statistics on World Population, GDP and Per Capita GDP, 1-2008 AD*. http://www.ggdc.net/MADDISON/oriindex.htm.

Mitchell, B.R. (2003), International Historical Statistics, Europe 1750-2000, Fifth Edition. Palgrave. Macmillan. New York.

Monash University (2012), "It's in our genes: why women outlive men," http://www.monash.edu.au/news/show/3970, accessed 5 August 2012.

OECD (2012), *OECD.Stat database*. Accessed on 09 May 2012.

Sicherl, P. (1973), "Time Distance as a Dynamic Measure of Disparities in Social and Economic Development," *Kyklos* XXVI(3): 559–575.

Sicherl, P. (1993), *Integrating Comparisons Across Time And Space, Methodology and Applications to Disparities within Yugoslavia.* Studies in Public Policy, No 213. Centre for the Study of Public Policy, University of Strathclyde, Glasgow.

Sicherl, P. (2004), *Time-Distance analysis: Method and applications.* eWISDOM, 2a/2004.

Sicherl, P. (2007), "The inter-temporal aspect of well-being and societal progress," *Social Indicators Research* 84: 231–247.

Sicherl, P. (1999), "A New View in Comparative Analysis", IB Revija, 1/1999, Ljubljana.

Sicherl, P. (2011), "New Understanding and Insights from Time-Series Data Based on Two Generic Measures: S-Time-Distance and S-Time-Step," *OECD Statistics Working Papers*, 2011/09. OECD Publishing, Paris. http://dx.doi.org/10.1787/5kg1zpzzl1tg-en.

Sicherl, P. (2012), *Time Distance in Economics and Statistics, New Insights from Existing Data.* Edition echoraum, Wien.

Sicherl P. (2013a), World Inequalities in Human Development Index (1980-2012), available on Amazon Kindle, B00HEHZ4SA and the printed version on CreateSpace eStore, 4623109

Sicherl, P. (2013b), Gender differences in life expectancy in the EU, IB Revija, XLVII, 2/2013.

Sicherl, P. (2013c), A geek's guide to measuring the MDGs, Guardian Professional, The Guardian, Friday 1 March 2013 12.48 GMT, web page http://www.guardian.co.uk/global-development-professionals-network/2013/feb/28/measuring-mdgs.

Sicherl, P. (in press), Inter-Temporal Aspect of Wellbeing. In A. C. Michalos (Ed.), Encyclopedia of Quality of Life and Well-Being Research. Dordrecht, Netherlands: Springer.

UN (2011), Department of Economic and Social Affairs, Population Division, *World Population Prospects: The 2010 Revision*, CD-ROM Edition.

UN (2013), Department of Economic and Social Affairs, Population Division, *World Population Prospects: The 2012 Revision*, DVD Edition.

UNDP (2007), United Nations Development Programme. "Women's political participation," *Human Development Report* 2007/2008, New York.

UNDP (2011), United Nations Development Programme. *Human Development Report* 2011, International Human Development Indicators, New York.

UNDP (2013a), *Human Development Report* 2013, The Rise of the South: Human Progress in a Diverse World, New York.

UNDP (2013b), UNDP web page. Accessed June 6, 2013. http://hdrstats.undp.org/en/tables/.

UNICEF (2013), Trends in infant mortality rates 1960-2011 (September 2012). www.childinfo.org.

LIST OF FIGURES AND TABLES

Figures

Tables

APPENDIX

Methodology

For methodology see freely available paper by Statistics Directorate, OECD:
P. Sicherl, New Understanding and Insights from Time-Series Data Based on Two Generic Measures: S-time-distance and S-time-step; Working paper No. 44, Statistics Directorate, OECD Publishing, Paris, November 2011.
Please download the paper on http://dx.doi.org/10.1787/5kg1zpzzl1tg-en.

More detailed methodological issues and numerous applications are available in the book:
Pavle Sicherl, Time Distance in Economics and Statistics, New Insights from Existing Data, p. 444, Echoraum, Vienna, 2012.
More information about the book is available on wikiprogress, http://www.wikiprogress.org/index.php/Time_Distance_in_Economics_and_Statistics.

The book is available on amazon.de, http://www.amazon.de/gp/product/3901941274.

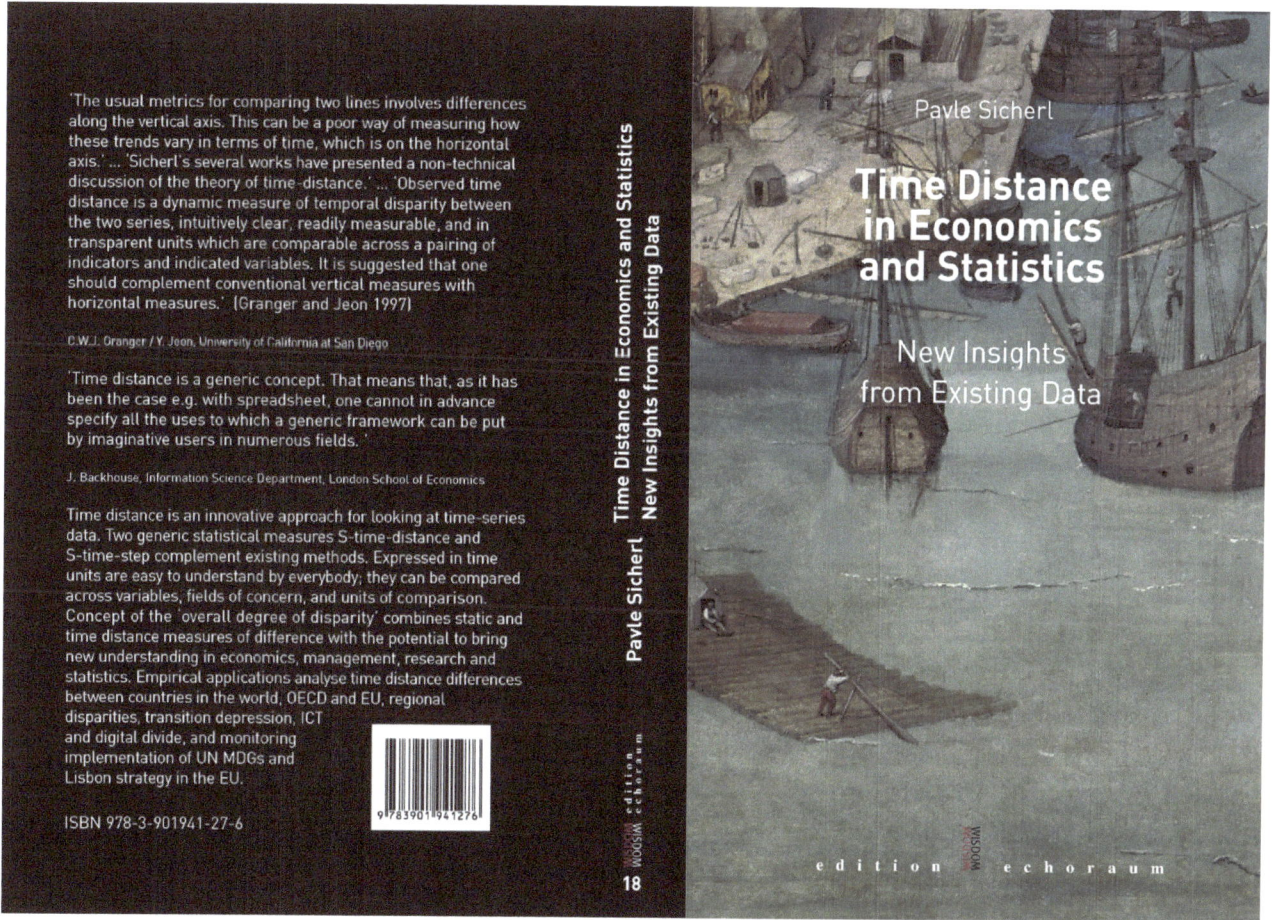

ABOUT THE AUTHOR

Professor Pavle Sicherl, Founder of SICENTER and principal researcher, 1993-present, Professor of Economics, University of Ljubljana, Slovenia (1975-2003); macroeconomic adviser in the Harvard University Development Advisory Service team in Ethiopia, (1970-1974); in 1960's Deputy Director of the Yugoslav Institute of Economic Research in Belgrade.

Born February 16, 1935 in Ljubljana, Slovenian citizen. Ph.D. (economics) and Dipl.Econ., University of Ljubljana; M.A. Development Economics (Williams College, MA, USA). Speciality: growth and inequality, he introduced new statistical measures, S-time-distance and S-time-step, to amend the present methods of analysing time-series data and disparities in many fields.

For this idea he received many fellowships and invitations: Senior Fulbright Research Award (Yale), London School of Economics, Institute of World Economics (Kiel), Institute for Advanced Studies (Vienna), etc. Visiting professor abroad, project leader for international and national projects, and consultant to the World Bank, OECD, UN, ILO, UNIDO, INSTRAW, ITU, EUROCHAMBRES.

Biography: Who's Who in the World, Marquis, 1991-1992 ... 2013.

Website: www.gaptimer.eu

Email: pavle.sicherl@gaptimer.eu